Spain. 1938. Oil on canvas, 36 x 23⅝ inches. Collection Edward James. The figures in the middle distance form the woman's head.

PAINTINGS DRAWINGS PRINTS

SALVADOR DALI

BY JAMES THRALL SOBY

THE MUSEUM OF MODERN ART, NEW YORK

CONTENTS

ACKNOWLEDGMENTS

I wish to thank the artist and his wife, who have supplied invaluable information about Dali's early career and have cooperated promptly and graciously since the exhibition was first planned. I wish also to thank Mr. Alfred H. Barr, Jr., Director of the Museum, for the kind attention he has given the text of this catalog and for the important suggestions he has made as to its content. Mr. Beaumont Newhall, Librarian of the Museum, has been of great assistance in compiling the bibliography, and the list of Dali's previous exhibitions is almost entirely the painstaking work of his staff. Mr. Monroe Wheeler, Director of Exhibitions and Publications, has been patient, considerate and helpful during the long course of the exhibition's preparation.

JAMES THRALL SOBY
Director of the Exhibition

LENDERS TO THE EXHIBITION

Mr. Walter C. Arensberg, Hollywood; Mr. and Mrs. R. Kirk Askew, Jr., New York; Mrs. George Waller Blow, New York; Mr. Joseph Cornell, Flushing, New York; Mrs. W. Murray Crane, New York; Mr. Salvador Dali, New York; Mr. Thomas A. Fransioli, Jr., New York; Mr. A. Conger Goodyear, Old Westbury, New York; Mr. Thomas Fine Howard, New York; Mr. Edward James, Beverly Hills, California; Mr. and Mrs. Sidney Janis, New York; Mrs. Gerard B. Lambert, Princeton, New Jersey; Mrs. David M. Levy, Mr. Julien Levy, New York; Mrs. Harold F. McCormick, Chicago; Mr. Henry P. McIlhenny, Germantown, Philadelphia; Dr. and Mrs. Leslie M. Maitland, Los Angeles; Mrs. G. Reginald Monkhouse, Cleveland, Ohio; Miss Ruth Page, Chicago; Mrs. John Pitney, Mendham, New Jersey; Mr. Allen Porter, New York; Mrs. Stanley B. Resor, New York; Mrs. Irving T. Snyder, Coronado, California; Mr. Edward M. M. Warburg, New York; Mr. Edward Wassermann, New York; Miss Vera Zorina, New York.

The Art Institute of Chicago; The Wadsworth Atheneum, Hartford, Connecticut; De Beers Consolidated Mines, Ltd., London; International Business Machines Corporation, New York; Verdura Incorporated, New York.

FOREWORD

The fame of Salvador Dali has been an issue of particular controversy for more than a decade. Our opinion of him differs from that of the public as reflected in the press and also, in some degree, from his own self-interpretation. At the conclusion of his text (page 30) Mr. Soby summarizes the significance of Dali's painting in relation to European culture and to present history. Mr. Soby, however, writes somewhat as the painter's spokesman, quoting him and carefully analyzing the influences under which his art has developed. For the reader who happens to be unfamiliar with the tenets and terminology of Surrealism, we should like therefore to give here the simplest possible statement of Dali's importance as we see it.

Dali's admirers as well as his detractors have sometimes regarded him as a master of the mere playfulness of art; one who has carried fantasy to the point of outrage; an odd kind of practical joker and scandalizer. No doubt he has encouraged this conception of himself and it may have worked to his advantage. Those critics and reporters who most indignantly decry his acts of eccentricity have done most for the reputation to which they object. Furthermore, Dali himself, fascinated by the revolution in psychology during the twentieth century, has constantly referred to himself as a paranoiac.

If this were simply so, our exhibition of his work, and the present volume, might seem inappropriate at a time like this. But we believe that the function of a museum now is two-fold, or three-fold. It must go on as usual, even at the risk of appearing to lack a tragic sense, so as to help maintain art and encourage artists through the crisis to a more propitious moment. It should also, when it can, exhibit works of art which show the relation of artists to the terrible events to which they are exposed along with everyone else. But there is another type of art which arises out of a troubled epoch which neither reports nor comments upon the trouble, but is in itself a significant happening in history; a sudden and perhaps unconscious revelation of the spirit of the day and age. We believe that Dali is an artist of the greatest interest at the moment, and meaningful in this historic sense. His imagination is not abnormal, at least no more so than that of a number of geniuses of painting in the past; no more so than the tormented psyche of today which is its basic theme. Is it not unreasonable for us to welcome revolutionary achievement in the sciences and then shudder at revolution in the realm of art? Dali's conduct may have been undignified, but the greater part of his art is a matter of dead earnest, for us no less than for him. The examples which Mr. Soby reproduces here were selected to assist the serious student who is more concerned with Dali's work than his behavior.

His lack of dignity, his instant appreciation of the sensibilities of the press, are indications of the timeliness of his mind, but go deeper than that. Mr. Soby has traced for us the influence of Vermeer on Dali, especially in the perfection of the latter's technique of painting. But Dali's general temper and subject matter are also rather similar to those of Jerome Bosch, the sixteenth-century Italian mannerists, and Jacques Callot. Think what went on in Europe between Bosch's birth and Callot's death. It was an era extraordinarily like ours. The Reformation and Counter-reformation altered everything for everyone. Rome was sacked and Vienna was besieged by the Turks. Politicians took over the Inquisition. The Jews were herded from country to country. The Spaniards under Alva were in the Netherlands with their Courts of Blood. As a modern historian has expressed it, "The air all over the continent blew dark from villages on fire, and resounded with screams, and stank of hungry children and sick women and cadavers of cavalry." Dali is the type of artist who is prescient about such things and his imagination is intoxicated by them. This is a day of wrath in many ways, and even in his youth Dali obviously saw it coming.

Certainly he offers no solution for the ills of the age. But we believe in lyricism as well as the more utilitarian functions of the creative spirit. Even excessive feeling in art is useful to humanity in crisis, in that it forces us to think. One thing we all understand now is that the optimism of the fortunate civilized nations has been of great peril to civilization. Dali's dream of the present is tragic, and we should not shrink from the shock and pain of it.

MONROE WHEELER

SALVADOR DALI

SALVADOR DALI was born on May 11, 1904, at Figueras, a small town near Barcelona where his father was a notary and a leading citizen. Dali was educated first in a public school, later in the private academy in Figueras conducted by the Brothers of the Marist Order. By his own account his childhood was extraordinarily violent, marked by fits of hysteria and acts of rage toward his family and his playmates. The megalomania which he now considers one of his primary creative assets was apparent in youth: on several occasions he flung himself down a stone staircase in the schoolyard in order to savor the frightened attention of his classmates. He was abnormally imaginative and he matured under the strain of a hypersensitivity to his surroundings. Yet like so many artists of our century, he has remained deeply in love with his own childhood; its terrors and quick ecstasies are re-experienced time and again in the paintings he has created as an adult. As a painter he has never ceased to affirm his birthright and the environment in which he grew up. The high pitch of Spanish emotion with its Inquisitional heritage of cruelty and pain, the Catalan love of fantasy and sanctification of instinct, are unmistakably reflected in his works. Moreover, the locale of a majority of his paintings is Spanish, whether it is the flat glaring terrain of the landscape near Barcelona, the beach at Rosas, or the rocky gorges of the upper Catalan country.

Unlike his famous countryman, Picasso, Dali was not a precocious artist in the sense of having early evolved a consistently mature style of painting. At twenty-two, an age at which Picasso had already begun to turn his back on the professional competence of his Blue Period, Dali was attending the School of Fine Arts in Madrid and had not yet decided what direction his art would take. Nevertheless, he had already been painting seriously for a long period and had passed through an astonishing series of artistic phases. Before he was ten years old he had completed two oil paintings, *Joseph greeting his brethren* and *Portrait of Helen of Troy*, ambitious subjects for a child, to say the least. Both paintings were executed in the style of the nineteenth century painters of genre scenes. The fact is interesting in view of Dali's later profession of respect for artists like Meissonier. It seems significant, too, that in reply to a question as to which Spanish painters he had admired most as a young man, Dali replied, "Modesto Urgell and Mariano Fortuny." He described the first of these two artists as "the Catalan Böcklin," the second as "the inventor of anecdotal colorism and the Meissonier of our country." Apparently even as a youth he felt a decided preference for those artists who had put a precise technique to story-telling purpose. It was a preference which was finally to bring him into sharp opposition to Picasso's generation, which had attempted to banish literature and history from the subject matter of painting.

During his adolescence Dali experimented with Impressionism and Pointillism (painting in little dots), having been influenced by an exhibition of late nineteenth century French art held at Barcelona and by the Impressionist paintings of the Spaniard, Ramon Pitchot. The period of his interest in Impressionism and its later ramifications was of relatively short duration, and

9

by the time he became a student in the Madrid School of Fine Arts he was in full and character-istically violent reaction against his own previous enthusiasm. On one occasion, when a student, he is said to have shown his contempt for the Impressionist tradition by winning a wager that he could paint a prize-winning Pointillist picture by splashing paint at a canvas from a distance of three feet. On another occasion when he and his classmates were told to look at a Gothic statue of the Virgin and paint exactly what they saw, Dali executed a picture of a pair of scales. To his irate teacher he explained, "Perhaps you see a Virgin like everyone else. I see a pair of scales" (bibl. 34). Thus were evinced in youth two qualities which largely account for the exceptional fame his art has since earned him: his technical virtuosity, and his insistence on painting the counter-appearances suggested to him by what he now calls his "paranoiac" processes of thought.

Sometime in the early 1920's, Dali's parents, returning from a visit to Paris, brought with them a catalog and manifesto of Italian Futurist art. Presumably these publications had been issued in Paris or Milan just prior to the World War, when Futurist activity had reached its climax. After perusing them Dali turned to the solution of the problems posed by the Futurist doctrine, using a technique in which traces of his earlier absorption in Pointillism still lingered. He was probably especially fascinated by the Futurists' attempts to suggest simultaneously various aspects of objects in motion, since these attempts are more than distantly related to his own preoccupation with multiple appearances of the same object. In Dali's case, as will presently be seen, the basis of interest in simultaneity has been psychological rather than kinetic, as it was among the Futurists. Yet the Futurists, no less than he, were intent upon amplifying tangible reality and proposed transfigurations in subject matter which presupposed an abnormal perception.

From an interest in Futurism Dali progressed, from 1923 to 1925, to an interest in the art of the *scuola metafisica*, the "Metaphysical School," which had had its most fruitful years in Rome, Florence and Milan from 1915 to 1920 under the guidance of Giorgio de Chirico and Carlo Carrà. Exactly how Dali came into contact with the painting of the *scuola metafisica* is not a matter of clear record. It seems probable, however, that paintings by de Chirico, Carrà and Giorgio Morandi had been exhibited in Madrid or Barcelona, and reproductions of them had certainly been circulated in Spain through the publications issued in Italy under the imprint *Valori Plastici*.

Dali's exposure to the art of the *scuola metafisica* was of paramount importance in his early career. The school's doctrine was eventually to swerve him from the abstract approach of the Cubist-Futurist tradition toward the Surrealist movement's concern with man's psychology. For the *scuola metafisica* had directly prefigured the reaction against purely abstract art which Surrealism in general and Dali in particular were to exemplify so forcefully. It had rejected Cubism as merely a late development of French Naturalism, concerned only with a plastic rearrangement of external appearances rather than with a reappraisal of these appearances. It had strongly opposed Futurism's ideological dependence on the concrete aspects of contemporary civilization; it had refuted Futurism's preoccupation with machines and machine-forms, an engrossing fact in view of Dali's later contempt for the industrialism of the twentieth century. The movement had proposed to explore the deeper roots of man's existence, to create an art of metaphysical incantation arising from inner perception and experience. It had emphasized the artist's salvation through

10

philosophical speculation, his comfort in the enigma, his retreat to the dream. However important the difference between its program and that of Surrealism, there can be no question that Dali was prepared for his career as a Surrealist by his eager adoption of the tenets of *pittura metafisica*.

These tenets were in essence a rationalization of the art which the school's greatest figure, Giorgio de Chirico, had achieved in the five years before the school had come into being. But oddly enough, considering the preponderant influence which de Chirico was later to have upon him, Dali at this time emulated Carrà's art more closely. During the years 1923–1925 he executed several still lifes which owe more to Carrà's technique than to that of de Chirico. They are marked by an emotive archaism peculiar to the former rather than to the latter, as may be seen in the *Still life* of 1924 herewith reproduced (page 33). The fact that Dali then chose Carrà instead of de Chirico as a master may account for the brief duration of his discipleship. For Carrà's painting of 1915–1918 was limited, as de Chirico's was not, by a dependence on what is now recognizable as a *poésie d'époque*. Sensing this fact, Dali soon decided that *pittura metafisica* was involved in non-pictorial considerations, already outworn. By 1925 he had disavowed it for experimentation with abstract art, deriving his inspiration at first from the late works of Cézanne, afterwards from the Cubist compositions of Picasso.

Dali's brief career as a Cubist is surprising in that it interrupted a trend toward the anti-abstract art which he was later to champion. Yet young artists of unmistakable originality have often ranged wide in faith during the period immediately prior to their adoption of a settled style. Furthermore, Dali had inevitably to face the issue which Cubism had raised in European art. Reduced to a dramatic decision, this issue consisted in whether a given younger artist should be for or against Picasso's dictates. Remembering that Picasso was a fellow Catalan, one can understand why Dali should have been caught, at some point, by the immense suction of his ideas. However, although Dali in his own words gave himself to Cubism "body and soul," although he showed remarkable virtuosity in painting Cubist works, he was not destined to paint permanently or even consistently in this vein. The little panel, *The basket of bread* (page 34), is dated 1926. It reveals that Dali had not lost touch with the realist tradition and that he aspired to a Dutch precision of technique during the very years when he was engrossed in Cubism. Painted fifteen years before *Two pieces of bread expressing the sentiment of love* (page 73), the panel exemplifies an equivalent ardor for objective clarity of statement. The panel is not isolated in his work of 1925–1927. To this period also belong portraits of his father and sister. Both portraits are entirely representational and free from Cubist distortion. In both, the figures are defined by the incisive contours he had come to admire in Ingres, whose influence on his drawing has persisted (page 78).

Sometime during 1928 Dali made a brief excursion to Paris, where he met Picasso. Prompted, perhaps, by his great countryman's lack of reverence for traditional media and inspired by the latter's *collages*, he returned home to execute several huge abstract canvases from which stones and all manner of heavy objects were suspended by thick cords. A few months later he returned to Paris for a second visit, during which he met and came under the influence of Miro, was introduced to Robert Desnos and Paul Eluard of the Surrealist group, and signed a contract with

11

the Goemans Gallery for an exhibition which he went home to prepare. For several months after his return to Spain he continued to work at abstractions on which the imprint of Miro's personality gradually superseded that of Picasso. This short period marks the last phase of Dali's interest in abstract art. Presently he was to react violently against this kind of art in general. By 1935 his book, *Conquest of the Irrational*, was to appear, containing a chapter entitled, "The Abject Misery of Abstraction-Creation." The chapter was to include the phrase, "this model mental debility called abstract art."

The signs of Dali's ultimate defection from the abstract movement were obvious by the summer of 1929. By then he had decided to apply what he knew to be an extraordinary manual dexterity to the exact transcription on canvas of his subconscious thoughts and dreams. By midsummer he had found his stride, painting *The lugubrious game* and *Accommodations of desire* (page 35). When his paintings began to arrive in Paris, it was clear that his sympathies lay with the Surrealists. A few weeks before his exhibition opened at the Goemans Gallery, André Breton, Surrealism's central figure, agreed to write the foreword to his catalog. On hearing Dali's decision to come to Paris to live, Breton appointed him an official Surrealist. Within a short time Dali was to become the movement's most spectacular exponent.

It was not the painter's technical gifts alone which won him prominence, although the draftsmanship in *Studies* (page 78) or the brushwork in *The feeling of becoming* (page 38) would probably earn an artist attention in any epoch. What distinguished him from established artists within the Surrealist group was his bringing to Surrealist art a new objectivity to replace the confessional subjectivity of his predecessors. He did so by changing the formula of creative stimulus. Whereas the art of the earlier Surrealists had sprung from an artificially induced and terminable state of receptivity to subconscious inspiration, Dali declared that his art sprang from a constant, hallucinatory energy. He proposed to paint like a madman rather than as an occasional somnambulist. He added that the only difference between himself and a madman was that he was not mad. But by simulating madness he professed himself able at will to proclaim the unreasonable with extreme conviction because his reason could be made to lose its power of objection. He made his purpose clear in his first book, *La femme visible*, published in 1930. "I believe the moment is at hand," he then wrote, "when by a paranoiac and active advance of the mind, it will be possible (simultaneously with automatism and other passive states) to systemize confusion and thus to help discredit completely the world of reality."

The history of art can furnish almost continuous precedent for Dali's reverence for madness, the most recent example being that of the nineteenth century Romantic artists who endowed the deranged mind with special allure. Yet there is a cardinal difference between Dali's attitude toward insanity and that of a Romantic like Géricault. Whereas Géricault had regarded madness as a phenomenon which was exotic precisely because it was impenetrable, Dali regarded it as an ideal state, to be entered into by the artist himself. He seems to have had no fear that, having identified himself with madness, his communication of its mysteries would be limited to the insane or to those with a scientific knowledge of insanity. In his *Declaration of the Independence of the Imagination and the Rights of Man to His Own Madness*, he later wrote: ". . . all men are equal in

12

De Chirico: *The Sailors Barracks*. 1914. Collection Henry Clifford.

De Chirico's pioneer use of deep perspective, sharp mysterious shadows, and evocative grouping of enigmatic or incongruous objects, influenced Dali in such works as those reproduced on pages 33, 34, 35, 36, 52 and 57.

their madness . . . madness (visceral cosmos of the subconscious) constitutes the common base of the human spirit."

Of Dali's early attempts at communicating his "paranoiac" visions, *Accommodations of desire* and *Illumined pleasures* (page 34) are typical and excellent examples. Both owe to Giorgio de Chirico an ideological debt which they share with nearly all Surrealist art. In neither picture is the technical influence of de Chirico so direct as in other paintings of the years 1929–1931, such as *The invisible man* (page 36), *Simulacrum of night* and *Vertigo*, yet this influence is nonetheless unmistakable in both. It was de Chirico who had reaffirmed deep perspective as a poetic instrument at a time when the Cubists were dismissing the third dimension as illusory or were representing it through a calligraphic shorthand. In *Accommodations of desire* and *Illumined pleasures*, Dali has utilized the recessive planes, abrupt scaling down of background objects and elongation of shadows through which, from 1911 to 1915, de Chirico had given his paintings of Italian squares an almost *trompe l'oeil* depth. Moreover Dali has borrowed from de Chirico an anti-naturalist manipulation of light to suggest the atmosphere of hallucination or dreams. In *Illumined pleasures* he has further adopted de Chirico's device of the boxed painting-within-the-painting, using it as a method of presenting successive aspects of dream imagery.

Here the resemblance between de Chirico's early paintings and those of Dali ends. For while de Chirico's art was basically concerned with a broad idealization of the process of dreaming, Dali's presented the scenario of a given "paranoiac" dream; while de Chirico had evoked the sensation of somnambulism in terms of lyric experience, Dali illustrated the details of a specific dream-continuity at a climax of its terrifying activity. In 1913 de Chirico had written: "What

13

I hear is worth nothing; there is only what I see with my eyes open and, even more, what I see with them closed." But what he had seen with his eyes closed had been the squares of Italy, arbitrarily transformed in accordance with the inner dictates of his inspiration, often ominous but always noble, elegiac and restrained. When Dali closed his eyes, it was to see a turbulent procession of images, indicative of all manner of psychic disturbance. Having read Freud with furious enthusiasm, he was no longer content, as de Chirico had been, to state the workings of the subconscious in general, poetic terms. Instead he wished to document these workings in full detail and with scientific accuracy. He was already what he afterwards declared all artists must become, "[a] carnivorous fish . . . swimming between two kinds of water, the cold water of art and the warm water of science" (bibl. 8).

Despite his belief in the constant inspirational force of his "paranoia," Dali shared the group Surrealist faith in sleep as an aid in distracting the vigil of conscious reason. Sleep, as he has since made clear in the canvas by that name (page 62), was to him a monster, because in their dreams men are free to commit the most hideous crimes; sleep was embryonic, because it gives men the warm shelter and immunity of the womb. Yet if a number of his early paintings are literal transcriptions of dreams, he nevertheless frequently relied on the waking inspiration of his "paranoiac" thought. He did so by recording the first image which occurred to him and then filling in the picture space with images suggested by this first image. Just as a true paranoiac is constantly seeing countless persecutory forms in whatever object is presented to his view, so Dali claimed that any given image suggested endless other images to him because of his "paranoiac" sensitivity. Applied to his painting, this theory meant that once his subconscious had supplied an initial form, the task of elaboration could be entrusted to conscious paranoiac reasoning. He defined the matter in *La femme visible* as follows: "The images which paranoiac thought may suddenly release will not merely spring from the unconscious; the force of their paranoiac power will itself be at the service of the unconscious."

Whether inspired by dreams or active paranoiac reasoning, Dali's paintings continued the restoration of the anecdote to art which the Dadaist works of Duchamp, Picabia and Max Ernst had initiated. He thus helped revive the theory of painting as an illustrative medium against which the Cubists had fought so relentlessly. (Following the lead of de Chirico and Ernst, he gave, and still gives, long descriptive titles to his paintings by contrast with the bare nomenclature of Cubist works.) The form which the anecdote took in his works was, of course, Freudian—that is, it was expressed in terms of symbolic appearances emerging from the dim, relatively unexplored regions of the subconscious. But in restoring the anecdote, whatever its form, Dali was obliged to face the limitation of all story-telling art: its tendency to become outmoded through later reactions against the literary, scientific or historical documentation which it has undertaken.

Dali proposed to transcend this limitation by the force of his revelations and by the precision with which he communicated them. He brought to the task an extremely fertile imagination which Picasso said reminded him of "an outboard motor continually running" (bibl. 9), and a clarity of technique already exhibited in *The basket of bread* of 1926. He called his technique "handmade photography," by which he meant to say that it defined appearances so sharply as

14

to make them rival those which, recorded by the camera, were indubitably existent. With him, in however temporary a sense, came to an end the reaction against painting as a photographic medium which had gathered force throughout the late nineteenth century and reached a climax in the early twentieth. Whereas André Derain, in describing his career as a Fauve, had written, "this was the epoch of photography . . . a fact which counted in our reaction against everything which resembled negatives taken from life," Dali went so far as to give his paintings a surface similar to that of glossy photographic prints. He wished, in a word, to depict the unreal with such extreme realism that its truth and validity could no longer be questioned.

In certain of his early canvases, among them *Accommodations of desire*, he adopted the Cubist practice of affixing real substances, or photographs and engravings of them, to his canvases. He did not do so in order to establish a link with reality, as the Cubists had done. Instead he intended to set the key for an over-all pattern of exactitude. Thus, in some of his early paintings, pasted-on engravings and photographs are supplemented by painted replicas so carefully executed as to be indistinguishable from the originals. In other pictures of the period, such as *Illumined pleasures*, forms are so painstakingly rendered as to startle the observer into a belief in the existence of the phenomena recorded. Just as ships within bottles have exaggerated identities as ships, because of their having been laboriously erected within so confined a space, so the objects in Dali's paintings were intended to have an added wonder because of their diminutive scale and completeness of detail.

At this juncture in his career Dali declared himself totally uninterested in the esthetic values of color and line, thus taking his place in the anti-artistic cycle which had begun so violently with the Dadaists. As already briefly noted, he admired painters of the past, particularly Meissonier, whose art was almost wholly notable for its photographic clarity of technique. He claimed to be completely indifferent to richness of pigment or elegance of contour. He not infrequently used offensive combinations of color; he often deliberately painted in the flat, unimaginative tones which popular artists employ in imitation of hand-tinted prints. In *Conquest of the Irrational* he gave his reasons for so doing. "The illusionism of the most abjectly *arriviste* and irresistible imitative art, the usual paralysing [sic] tricks of *trompe l'oeil*, the most analytically narrative and discredited academicism," he wrote, "can all become sublime hierarchies of thought and the means of approach to new exactitudes of concrete irrationality." What alone interested him was the quality of his obsessions and the means of their literal transcription. "My whole ambition in the pictorial domain," as he put the matter, "is to materialize the images of concrete irrationality with the most imperialist fury of precision" (bibl. 8).

In the above-mentioned paintings of 1929 and in other outstanding canvases of that year— *The lugubrious game, Portrait of Paul Eluard, The first days of spring*—occur many of the iconographical devices which were to haunt his art for many years. The foetal creature which lies in the foreground of *The persistence of memory* (page 39) begins as the profile of a woman in both *Illumined pleasures* and *The lugubrious game*. In the two last-named paintings, as in a majority of his early works, appears the female praying mantis, an insect endeared to the artist by its habit of devouring the male immediately following the act of procreation. The pictures in general are crowded

15

with implements of persecution, particularly with sharp instruments symbolic of mutilation; they swarm with fetishes direct from Krafft-Ebing's case histories—slippers, keys, hair and so on. They are, moreover, largely concerned with what Dali called the three cardinal images of life: excrement, blood and putrefaction. In contrast to Miro's paintings, which are primarily notable for the over-all impact they achieve when seen as a group, each of Dali's works is individual in quality and specific in intent. Those who object to them on the grounds that they are scatologic, sacrilegious and ugly, would hear no dissent from Dali himself. "It has to be said once and for all to art critics, artists &c.," he wrote, "that they need expect nothing from the new Surrealist images but disappointment, distaste and repulsion" (bibl. 2). In painting these images he was attempting to release the dark, repressed poetry of the subconscious. He had previously accepted without reservation André Breton's definition of Surrealism as "thought's dictation, all exercise of reason and every esthetic or moral preoccupation being absent."

Shortly after his arrival in Paris Dali evolved what he later called "the paranoiac-critical method" and defined as a "spontaneous method of irrational knowledge based upon the inter- pretive-critical association of delirious phenomena" (bibl. 8). Reduced to simpler terms, the method consisted in a critical approach to accepted truths and appearances which substituted for the traditional concept of their meaning a new concept, often diametrically opposite and based primarily on psychological research. Thus far the method is clearly Freudian in inspiration. But to Freud's system of dispassionate psychoanalysis, Dali added an implemental force which he considered his own: his ability spontaneously to recognize hidden, associated meanings because of his "paranoiac" sensitivity. He presently began to apply the method to the sanctified and the obvious and to probe for evidence of a reverse meaning long concealed from normal vision. The results of his scrutiny were immediately reflected in his painting.

The first of the several thematic obsessions which the "paranoiac-critical method" led him to record was concerned with the legend of William Tell. In accordance with his "paranoiac-criti- cal" standards of interpretation, the legend was drastically re-read. It became not a legend of filial devotion, but one of incestuous mutilation, and as René Crevel wrote in *Dali ou l'anti-obscu- rantisme*, "As Freud resuscitated Oedipus, he (Dali) resuscitated William Tell." Dali utilized his interpretation of the legend for the libretto of a ballet, published in his book, *Babaouo*, in 1932. Beginning in 1930 with *William Tell* and ending in 1934 with the large panel, *The enigma of William Tell*, the legend supplied the subject for a number of his most important paintings, among them *The old age of William Tell* (page 41), one of the finest works of his career. In these paintings the subject of mutilation is treated in varying degrees of symbolic disguise. The theme itself is embroidered with a frieze of objects which had become obsessive for the artist: fried eggs on a platter, limp watches, swarming ants and so on.

A second and equally lasting thematic obsession reflected in his art was supplied by his re- appraisal of Millet's famous painting, *The Angelus*, as a monument to sexual repression. To Dali's mind the picture's pious subject matter served merely as an outer disguise to a vicious, instinctive energy which he considered truly poetic. Like the other Surrealists he preferred passion to restraint, desire to its sublimation, the black, erotic power of the subconscious to the cool equivo-

16

cation of reason. Not unmindful that *The Angelus* was widely regarded as a sacred image, he used its bowed figures as symbols of a furious counter-reality concealed from normal vision by a superficially devout iconography. The *Angelus* figures appear in a number of his paintings executed between 1932 and 1935, among them those here reproduced on pages 45 and 56. He also included the figures in concrete reconstructions of dream imagery which he called "Surrealist objects operating symbolically." Following the line of Freud's research on the hidden forms in Leonardo's *Virgin on the lap of Saint Ann*, he explored what he considered to be the erotic origin of Millet's inspiration in general (bibl. 21).

Meanwhile, his art was affected by more purely esthetic influences. Certain of Max Ernst's poetic devices impressed him and in 1930 his painting drew close to that of the young French Surrealist, Yves Tanguy. In *The font* (page 37) the ball-like forms on the marble floor suggest Tanguy's curious images, while the general tonality has the shimmering iridescence of the latter's works of this period. Moreover, the tilted, broad perspective of Dali's canvas, scattered with minute objects which cast heavy shadows, is closely allied to that in such Tanguy paintings as the Museum of Modern Art's *Mama, Papa is wounded!* of 1927. Tanguy had in turn inherited his interest in deep perspective from de Chirico, but he had used perspective in a manner which, by comparison with that of de Chirico, was rather more abstract and more freely atmospheric. Dali followed Tanguy's example. In his paintings of 1930 and 1931 space is manipulated to suggest an infinity against which the drama of his objects and figures is projected. Yet the objects themselves, with exceptions such as the object on the ground in *Shades of night descending* (page 42), are usually readily identifiable, while those of Tanguy are not. From the meeting of Psychoanalysis and Morphology, later celebrated in one of Dali's canvases (page 70), Psychoanalysis had already emerged triumphant.

The influence of Tanguy was supplemented by that of *art nouveau* architecture and decoration. Having expressed a dislike for abstract art, Dali also dismissed modern architecture in favor of what he was presently to call the "undulant-convulsive" style which had been evolved at the end of the previous century (bibl. 10). He came by this preference more or less naturally. In Catalan Spain he had been surrounded by the architectural fantasies of the style's most astonishing practitioner, Antoni Gaudí. Indeed, it seems safe to assume that Dali's enthusiastic familiarity with Gaudí's works had been a determining factor in his decision to become himself a champion of the irrational and the fantastic. Certainly it now prompted his contempt for what he described as the "hyper-materialism" of contemporary architecture as this architecture had been defined by Le Corbusier, Gropius, Oud, Miës van der Rohe and their disciples. Dali was not, of course, the only artist in Paris to avow this distaste, since the younger Surrealists and the Neo-Romantic artists shared his feeling, while Picasso, Matisse and other leaders of the older generation had been apathetic toward the achievements of even the greatest modern architects. Yet Dali was more extreme in his belief than any of these men, and perhaps the only one capable of saying, "For one thing is certain: I hate simplicity in all its forms" (bibl. 8). He was also the first, as he later pointed out, to take *art nouveau* architecture seriously as an antidote to contemporary building. (He took it so seriously, in fact, that he wished to pursue his identification with it to the point of

17

Art nouveau forms which influenced Dali in such pictures as *The Invisible Man* (page 36) and *The Font* (page 37). *Left:* Ornament from entrance to Paris subway, 1900. *Right: Art nouveau* bust. Both from Dali: *De la beauté terrifiante et comestible de l'architecture "modern' style"* (bibl. 10).

eating it.) The degree of his isolation from the esthetic theory then current may be measured by the fact that in 1929, the year of his arrival in Paris, a magazine of advanced Parisian taste, *Cahiers d'Art*, had described Gaudì as the architect who had utterly ruined the city of Barcelona.

The influence of *art nouveau* architecture and ornamentation on Dali's art was a broad one and profoundly affected his visual habits, especially during the years 1930–1934. Many of the ecto-plasmic forms which haunt his works of this period are based upon the "undulant-convulsive" style of *art nouveau* decorative busts or of the ornamentation of the Paris subway stations and of Gaudì's façades in Barcelona, as may be seen in *The font*. Although the influence cannot often be so directly traced and segregated, it largely accounts for the metal torso and its appendages in *The Javanese mannequin* (page 47). In the few sculptures which Dali executed during this period, among them *Hysterical and aerodynamic feminine nude* of 1934, he appears to have been inspired equally by *art nouveau* forms and by the Futurist sculpture of Boccioni, for which he has on several occasions expressed a deep admiration.

From the beginning of his career Dali has evaded questions as to the meaning of his paintings by stating that he does not know what their meaning is. No one, he adds, is more astonished by the images which appear on his canvases than he; and having created them, he feels that his responsibility toward them is ended. Nevertheless his writings at times furnish partial data on the iconography of certain paintings, as in the case of *The persistence of memory* (page 39) and *The spectre of sex appeal* (page 48). Of the former picture he has written, with a glance at Einstein which the great physicist has not yet returned: "be persuaded that Salvador Dali's famous limp watches are nothing else than the tender, extravagant and solitary paranoiac-critical camembert of time and space" (bibl. 8). Although precisionists in psychological discussion may find the sentence equivocal, to put it mildly, the word "camembert" furnishes a clue to one of the painter's most fervid obsessions—his preoccupation with malleability, his passion for *softness*, which leads him to convert hard objects, like watches, into substances as soft as camembert. Furthermore, in *La femme visible* he had previously written that rotting flesh covered with ants could have "the hard and blinding flash of new gems," were it not for the intervention of one's awareness of time. In *The persistence of memory* time has gone limp, and the ants on the watch in the foreground have the glitter of rare jewels.

The ideological inspiration for *The spectre of sex appeal* has also been described in part by the artist. "I am very proud," he wrote, "of having predicted in 1928, at the height of the cult for functional and practical anatomy, in the midst of the most shocking scepticism, the imminence of the round and salivary muscles of Mae West, viscous and terrible with hidden biological meanings. Today I announce that all the new sexual allure of women will come from the possible utilization of their capacities and resources as ghosts, that is to say, their possible dissociation, their charnel and luminous decomposition" (bibl. 25). He added that the woman with sex appeal would henceforth be demountable, as the figure in *The spectre of sex appeal* quite clearly is, so that she could satisfy her profound exhibitionism by detaching various sections of her anatomy and passing them around to be admired separately. It has also been his conviction that bones should be worn outside rather than beneath the flesh, a conviction absolutely opposed to that of one of his idols, Ingres, who was so terrified of bones that he was at pains to cover them with ample flesh and almost to deny their structural function in anatomy. Dali consequently conceived of the ghost of sex appeal as composed of protruding bones and stuffed, detachable forms held in place by crutches which he defined in the *Dictionnaire abrégé du surréalisme* as "wooden supports deriving from Cartesian philosophy. Generally used as a support for the tenderness of soft structures." The ghost is painted in more brilliant colors than he had ever before used, because it must be "more beautiful and terrifying than the white truffle of death: a rainbow" (bibl. 25).

Dali's preoccupation with bones reached a climax in 1933 and 1934 when he executed a series of paintings in which all manner of bone distortions, chiefly cephalic, are exhaustively treated. The inspiration for the series may have come from a childhood memory of a man suffering from hydrocephalus. It is surely no mere coincidence, however, that for several years prior to 1933, Picasso had been engrossed in osseous formations and deformations. Since Dali's arrival in Paris his respect for his compatriot had steadily become more pronounced. By 1933 Picasso was on intimate terms with the Surrealists, and since his latest works were the subject of almost daily discussion among them, it seems reasonable to suppose that Dali's bone series was at least partially inspired by that of Picasso. Whatever their derivation, *Myself at the age of ten when I was the grasshopper child* (page 43) and *Average atmospherocephalic bureaucrat in the act of milking a cranial harp* (page 49) are key examples of a series which reached its high point in *The invisible, fine and average harp*. It is perhaps unnecessary to point out that Dali's preoccupation with harps is in part motivated by his admiration for Harpo Marx, of whom he has made many drawings (page 81).

19

There is evidence that Dali's contempt for purely esthetic values in painting had begun to weaken by late 1933. *The phantom cart* (page 44) of that year was succeeded in 1934, 1935 and 1936 by the series of beach scenes at Rosas which included *Paranoiac-astral image* (page 55) and *Noon* (page 58). All three of the above-named pictures are notable for a new and deliberate lyricism; all are luminous in tone, their subtle gradations of color a far cry from the hard cacophony of "handmade photography." Yet the change they illustrate is not one of technique alone. By comparison with *The spectre of sex appeal* these paintings reveal that the artist could sometimes abandon his ideological dramatics to attain a more dulcet poesy. He obviously did so only temporarily, since in 1936 he was to paint *Soft construction with boiled beans; premonition of civil war* (page 61), possibly the most savage and relentlessly psychopathic of all his works. But for a time, at least, he was content to record a quieter inspiration. In *The phantom cart*, the contours of the wagon merge with those of the town toward which it is traveling, so that by an appealing poetic *tour de force* the cart becomes its own destination. In paintings of the Rosas series, too, sentiment is granted a new importance. Returning to the seashore which he had visited in youth, Dali painted the series of pictures, relatively free of Freudian connotation, in which the central figures are those of himself as a child and of his childhood nurse.

Apart from *Paranoiac-astral image* and *Noon*, the series included, among other paintings, *Apparition on the beach at Rosas* and *Paranoiac-medianimic image*. Dali described the figures in all these pictures as "instantaneous," by which he meant that they were intended to have the hallucinatory appearance of stereoscopic images projected briefly against a prepared background. Precisely what stimulated the artist's interest in figures of the kind is difficult to say, although precedent for his interest may certainly be found. Nearly a hundred years before, Gustave Courbet had given certain of his figures a weirdly fleeting connection with the landscape, a procedure which led Giorgio de Chirico to declare that Courbet's figures "do not appear in their current guise (verism), but in their poetic and phantasmal aspect (realism)." Perhaps following Courbet's example, Christian Bérard in 1933 painted a series of beach scenes in which a sense of dislocation between the figures and the landscape is purposefully conveyed for phantomic effect. But while Bérard's influence on Dali has become recognizable in very recent years, there is no reason to suppose that it was felt as early as 1934–1936. Moreover, perhaps the nearest equivalent to Dali's "instantaneous" figures is not to be found in the art of either Courbet or Bérard, but in that of the Englishman, William Dyce, whose *Pegwell Bay* (1858) Dali could not have seen at that time. Dali did not go to England until after his Rosas series was well begun, and even then was almost exclusively preoccupied with the Pre-Raphaelites, whose works he found "paranoiac" in every detail (bibl. 36). It therefore seems likely that he was impelled to paint his series by the simple fact of his having spent a vacation at Rosas where figures appeared like ghosts in the brilliant seashore light. A painter of original and highly personal vision, Dali has seldom had to go beyond his own feverish imagination for inspiration. The point must be emphasized here, lest a discussion of parallels between his art and that of other painters be taken to signify that he has been an imitative or eclectic artist. Whatever accusations may be brought against him, this one surely cannot be among them. On the contrary, his individuality is so pronounced that its effect on present-day

20

esthetics is widely discernible, surviving drastic adaptation and dilution at the hands of lesser artists.

Although the costumes worn by the figures in the Rosas series can probably be ascribed to the period 1905–1910, in inspiration they belong to the nineteenth century, and at this juncture it may be well to mention Dali's growing devotion to certain aspects of that century's Romantic tradition. While French Romanticism seems to have impressed him little, except for such untypical manifestations as Lautréamont's *Chants de Maldoror* and the Louvre's Delacroix, *Still life with lobsters,* he has been more and more attracted to German Romanticism. One of his paintings of the Rosas period bears the revelatory title, *Instantaneous presence of Ludwig II of Bavaria, Salvador Dali, Lenin and Wagner on the beach at Rosas.* If the name of Lenin was included out of deference to Surrealism's Communist platform, that of Wagner was included for abidingly personal reasons. For Wagner was, and remains, the painter's favorite composer by far. The music for Dali's ballet, *Bacchanale* (1939), is of course from the Venusberg scene in *Tannhäuser.* A second ballet, *Mad Tristram,* as yet unproduced, is based upon music from *Tristan und Isolde,* and there is no reason to doubt that Dali will some day suggest costumes, décor and choreographic action to accompany other Wagnerian music. The life of Wagner's mad patron, Ludwig II of Bavaria, has enthralled the painter, furnishing the central theme for his ballet, *Bacchanale,* as well as several episodes utilized in his art. Like de Chirico before him, Dali has also been absorbed in Nietzsche's thunderous message, and again following de Chirico's lead, he has acclaimed Arnold Böcklin as one of the master artists of all time. On his first visit to America in 1934, he was so moved by the Metropolitan Museum's Böcklin, *Isle of the Dead,* that he returned home to paint *Interior court of the 'Isle of the Dead'* and *Fountain of Böcklin.*

As a natural complement to the widening cultural allusion in Dali's art, the painter has come gradually to admire past artists in whom he had previously shown little interest. Although he continues to hail Meissonier as a great master, perhaps he has recently done so for the shock value which such a profession of respect cannot fail to have upon a generation trained to regard Meissonier as the epitome of the false-artistic. The painters whose art he has more seriously venerated of late are of a different order. Chief among them are Velasquez and Vermeer of Delft, whom he has described as "the great Realist painters" (bibl. 8). The hard, broad modeling of Velasquez' early period, spent under the influence of Caravaggio, has been used by Dali in many works, of which *Impression of Africa* (page 64) and *Philosophy illuminated by the light of the moon and the setting sun* (page 71) are the most conspicuous examples. The influence of Velasquez' later paintings on Dali is no less marked. It accounts in good part for the greater textural brilliance of more recent canvases by comparison with earlier paintings. In *Cardinal, cardinal!* (page 54), for example, the foreground figures, whose featureless heads resemble those of de Chirico's mannequins of 1915, are painted with a glittering impasto which seems specifically related to Velasquez' late technique. And if in recent works Dali has continued to employ the bland finish of "handmade photography," in a number of them he has used it as a foil to passages of radiant and thick texture. *Apparition of face and fruit-dish on a beach* (page 69) typifies his new, contrapuntal manipulation of pigment. Its broad glossy areas are broken at intervals by a richness of surface and tone which harks back to Velasquez' opulent handling of Spanish costume.

21

Dali's respect for the art of Jan Vermeer can only be described as obsessive. He has painted Vermeer's ghost (page 53); he has utilized the Rijksmuseum's *Young girl reading* as the basic theme of his own *The image disappears*, in which Vermeer's young girl is metamorphosed into a man with a beard; he has made Vermeer's "trade mark," the pearl, a symbol of cancerous beauty which that martyr-artist, the oyster, creates out of the slow irritation which may cause its death. At various times in his career he has declared that his ultimate ambition is to be able to paint like Vermeer, and having learned that an aged woman in Vienna had after forty years mastered the art of perfectly imitating Vermeer's technique, he prepared to visit her, only to learn that she had been driven away by Hitler's invading armies. His debt to Vermeer is not only avowed but apparent. It accounts for the yellow, pink and blue tonality of certain sections in his more recent paintings and for the quality of precision with which such a picture as *Two pieces of bread expressing the sentiment of love* (page 73) is handled.

Both *The ghost of Vermeer of Delft, which can be used as a table* (page 53) and *The weaning of furniture-nutrition* (page 54) illustrate a fundamental facet of Dali's "paranoia": his belief that the animate and the inanimate are interdependent in significance and function, with the inanimate taking its vitality from its relation to the living or from a strange capacity to come alive. Thus the leg of Vermeer's ghost serves as a table, while the chest of drawers in *The weaning of furniture-nutrition* owes its existence to the human nurse from whose back it has come and from whom it has itself derived the power to give birth to an infant chest of drawers. The most plausible basis for Dali's strange treatment of inanimate objects lies in his very obvious loathing of all mechanical things and forms, a loathing he expressed in his *Declaration of the Independence of the Imagination and the Rights of Man to His Own Madness*, wherein he advised his fellow-artists: "Only the violence and duration of your hardened dream can resist the hideous mechanical civilization that is your enemy . . ." An anti-mechanist in general philosophy, he has also been anti-mechanical in esthetics. The absolute opposite of an artist like Léger, who has drawn inspiration from contemporary machinery, Dali has consistently urged painters to turn their backs on the lifeless externals of modern civilization. "The history of the true creative artist," he has written, "is filled with the abuses and encroachments by means of which an absolute tyranny is imposed by the industrial mind over the new creative ideas of the poetic mind" (bibl. 11).

As already briefly noted, Dali's dislike for industrialism and its products may have been inherited from the artists of the *scuola metafisica* by whom he was influenced in youth. Yet his own reaction has been far more excessive than theirs. The signs of his contempt for the inanimate and the mechanical are many and characteristically extravagant. He has carried this contempt to the point of surrounding himself with furniture converted to living shapes: a sofa made to resemble Mae West's lips; a telephone concealed within a plaster lobster, "cold, green and aphrodisiac as the augur-troubled sleep of the cantharides" (bibl. 11). As part of his attempt to animate the lifeless, he has designed necklaces and bracelets which rotate slowly on their wearer's neck or arm, bringing into view a series of scabrous images. In the paintings *Palladio's corridor of Thalia* (page 63) and *Palladio's corridor of dramatic surprise* (page 67), he has changed to human form the stage properties through which Palladio achieved the astonishing foreshortening

22

The caprices and ingenious tricks of Mannerist artists and ornament designers of the period 1550–1650 were adapted by Dali for more serious purposes.

Arcimboldo, a master of double or composite images like the *Head-Landscape* on page 24 (turn the page to see the head) may have influenced Dali in such works as those reproduced on pages 36, 69, and 74.

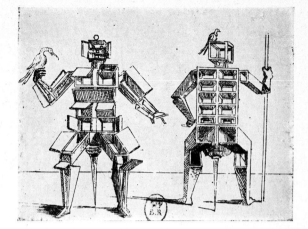

Above: the "furniture-figures" invented by Bracelli, another Mannerist artist, in his series of *Capricci* or *Bizarie* of 1624, influenced Dali directly in his *Weaning of furniture-nutrition* (page 54) and *Figure of drawers* (page 82).
Left: The ribbon figure at the left of Dali's *The triumph of Nautilus* (page 75) seems derived from Bracelli's ribbon figures. (See bibl. 64a: items 5, 6, 53, 320, 323.)

of his setting for the *Teatro Olimpico* in Vicenza. Wherever possible Dali has made living organisms usurp, jeopardize or obviate the function of machinery and machine products; whenever possible, he has forced the inanimate to take part in action for which the essential requisite is animation itself. The tendency is further illustrated by such a painting as *Debris of an automobile giving birth to a blind horse biting a telephone* (page 66). The automobile is here given the ability to reproduce not itself but the horse, which in contemporary civilization it has nearly driven out of existence, but which now seems to emerge triumphant from the wreck of industrialism. The horse releases its fury by biting a telephone, a mechanical instrument which Dali considers so disastrous in connotation that at the time of the Munich Conference, arranged by telephone, he made the instrument the iconographical center of several paintings, among them *Imperial violets* and *The sublime moment* (page 65).

As far back as 1929 Dali had begun work on *The invisible man* (page 36), a major work in his career which was not completed until 1933. The picture furnishes proof, reinforced by his writings, that from the very beginning of his connection with Surrealism he has been fascinated

Arcimboldo, Tradition of: *Landscape—head* (double image). Late sixteenth century.

by a visual phenomenon which has played an important part in the iconography of his paintings. This phenomenon is the double image—that is, the image which suggests or turns into a second image either at first glance or on being stared at intently. The phenomenon has been experienced by artists and laymen through the centuries. In painting, it was elaborately exploited by fantasists of the sixteenth and seventeenth centuries, among them Arcimboldo and Bracelli, by whom Dali claims his own interest in the phenomenon to have been directly inspired. For the Romantics of the nineteenth century, the double image held a special fascination. Early in the century, Delacroix made drawings of a lion's paw which turned into a human hand; at the century's end, Odilon Redon wrote in *À soi-même:* "The sense of mystery is always to be found in the equivocal, in double and triple aspects, suspicions of aspects (images within images), and in forms which are beginning to be or will begin to be, according to the state of mind of the observer." Popular artists, among them our own Currier and Ives, utilized the phenomenon in making picture puzzles, concealing almost endless images within the pattern of given subject matter. But Dali has gone further than any of his predecessors. He has not adopted the double image as a *jeu d'esprit*, as the fantasists and popular artists did, nor has he been content to share

24

the Romantics' conception of it as merely mysterious. Instead, he has proclaimed that the second, hallucinatory image suggested by a given object may be reality itself. In discussing multiple images in *La femme visible* he wrote: "I challenge materialists . . . to inquire into the more complex problem as to which of these images has the highest probability of existence if the intervention of desire is taken into account."

Dali believes that paranoiacs have a special capacity for the recognition of double images inasmuch as their disordered minds are hypersensitive to hidden appearances, real or imagined. That his own capacity for their recognition is extraordinary, no one can in fairness deny. On numerous occasions he has proved it beyond doubt, as when he discovered that the head in one of Picasso's paintings, on being turned sideways, almost exactly paralleled the image of an African village on a postcard in his own possession. (He painted a picture combining the images, entitled *The paranoiac face.*) He early defined the double image in terms of its reproduction in art as "such a representation of an object that it is also, without the slightest physical or anatomical change, the representation of another entirely different object, the second representation being equally devoid of any deformation or abnormality betraying arrangement" (bibl. 2). In *The invisible man* and *Invisible sleeping woman, horse, lion* of 1930, he showed great ingenuity and imaginative skill in depicting double images in accordance with this definition, in both cases recording a dual identity which has a definite basis in abnormal psychology—a woman turning into a horse or lion.

In earlier paintings such as these, Dali was content to present two, or at most three, images in one. In the text of *La femme visible*, however, he made clear that he considered this numerical limitation arbitrary. "The double image," he wrote, ". . . may be extended, continuing the paranoiac advance, and then the presence of another dominant idea is enough to make a third image appear . . . and so on, until there is a number of images limited only by the mind's degree of paranoiac capacity." As his technique became more flexible, he consequently extended the sequence of images-within-images until in paintings such as *Apparition of face and fruit-dish on a beach* (page 69) he arrived at an astonishingly intricate succession of appearances and counter-appearances. By contrast with the Cubists, who had reduced the subject in painting to a minor and sometimes non-existent status, Dali provided his pictures with a sequence of subjects, each of them equally important and all of them interdependent. He reached a climax of complexity with *The endless enigma* of 1939, a canvas in which no less than six large-scale images are contained within the same over-all composition. Since that time the painter has returned to a simpler handling of the phenomenon of multiple images, as in such recent canvases as *Old age, adolescence, infancy* (page 74). Perhaps his most brilliant application of multiple images is to be found in *Spain* (frontispiece), surely a picture destined for a high place in the history of the art of today.

The face of the central figure in *Spain* is defined by episodes from a cavalry combat after Leonardo, and it should here be mentioned that the Renaissance master belongs to the incongruous company of heroes celebrated in Dali's "paranoiac-critical" approach to esthetics. The reasons for his inclusion are evident. As already noted, Leonardo's iconography had been the subject of analysis by Dali's mentor, Sigmund Freud. Then the painter himself discovered that

"Leonardo proved an authentic innovator of paranoiac painting by recommending to his pupils that, for inspiration, in a certain frame of mind they regard the indefinite shapes of the spots of dampness and the cracks on the wall, that they might see immediately rise into view, out of the confused and the amorphous, the precise contours of the visceral tumult of an imaginary equestrian battle" (bibl. 9). Hence the cavalry combat used in *Spain* has become what the figures from Millet's *Angelus* were in earlier Dali paintings: a symbolic reference to an ideology which the artist finds related and sympathetic to his own. The combat has provided the theme of numerous drawings (pages 79 and 80). Dali's recent works also testify that his admiration for Leonardo has not been merely ideological. The enigmatic face of da Vinci's Madonnas is utilized for the foreground figure in *Inventions of the monsters* (page 62) and recurs in other canvases, while Leonardo's technical influence on Dali's draftsmanship is in certain cases unmistakable.

Simultaneously with his development of the multiple image, Dali has adapted to his own use a related visual phenomenon: that of the object which, once seen, recurs in the imagination time and again, sometimes varying as to identity and scale but always remaining the same in general outline. For want of a better term, the phenomenon may be called that of the repetitive form. It has been more or less widely experienced, since nearly everyone has at times been troubled by a shape which recurs everywhere, assuming inexplicable guise. Dali has recorded his own "paranoiac" sensitivity to the phenomenon in a number of paintings. Thus in *The weaning of furniture-nutrition* the chest of drawers leaves its own outline in the nurse's back and in turn gives birth to a smaller chest identical in shape. In *Nostalgic echo* (page 57) the bell in the tower becomes in succession a girl skipping rope, a keyhole in the chest of drawers, and a shadowy figure standing under the far arcade. As in the case of the multiple image, Dali believes the recognition of repetitive images to be limited only by "paranoiac" capacity.

In the years immediately prior to the outbreak of the present war Dali made three extended visits to Italy. The effect of these visits has been increasingly evident in his painting. Not only has close familiarity with the great Italian tradition still further moderated his disdain for established esthetic standards, but the impact of this tradition has altered and widened his own technical means. To his list of preferred painters of the past must now be added a new galaxy: Botticelli, whose *Birth of Venus* was later to be emblazoned across the façade of Dali's Dream House at the World's Fair in New York; Piero di Cosimo, who in Dali's words "observed the viscous and mucous and bloody contours of tuberculer [sic] spit, that there might rise into view enigmatic and atavistic compositions, fire and the horrible dragon of the oyster" (bibl. 9); Raphael, whose figures de Chirico had described as phantasmal and statuesque, and whose *St. George and the dragon* Dali considers the finest painting in America; and Uccello, long since hailed as a precursor of Surrealism by André Breton himself. Apart from these and other masters of the Renaissance, he has developed a new esteem for painters of Mannerism and the Baroque. Caravaggio has joined Vermeer and Velasquez in the inner circle of his idols, and both *Impression of Africa* and *Philosophy illuminated by the light of the moon and the setting sun*, however close to the early Velasquez in spirit, relate back to Caravaggio himself in their dramaturgy and in the bold handling of their foreshortening and chiaroscuro. *Debris of an automobile giving birth to a blind horse*

26

biting a telephone, whatever its relation to a passage in Picasso's *Guernica*, has a definite affinity to the jeweled night scenes of the Baroque tradition.

The influence of the Baroque is particularly noticeable in *Palladio's corridor of Thalia, Palladio's corridor of dramatic surprise* and *Group of women imitating the gestures of a schooner* (page 72). The first two pictures are exuberantly handled, with obvious relish in values of impasto, and their long, slashing high lights suggest the technique of Magnasco. In the last-named canvas the background figure, constructed of circular brushstrokes, seems directly inspired by Bracelli's figures composed of typographers' scrolls, while the rushing tension between the foreground figures is prefigured in certain paintings of the Italian Baroque such as Guido Reni's famous *Atalanta and Hippomenes*. But if the frenzied motion of all three paintings relates them to the Baroque, their elegant elongation of forms derives from pre-Baroque Mannerism. It seems likely, however, that Dali's Mannerist distortions have been adapted from Spanish rather than Italian sources, since they predate his absorption in sixteenth-century Italian art. Just as Picasso in youth had borrowed stylistic devices from Morales, El Greco and other Spanish artists of the Mannerist tradition, so Dali from the very beginning of his career has come under the influence of native Mannerism. This influence may be detected in the exaggerated muscularity and diminutive feet of the figures in the right background of *The old age of William Tell* (page 41), and it recurs at intervals throughout his work. In certain of his most recent paintings the dominant style is that of Mannerism turned "psychological," in the contemporary sense of the latter term.

Dali's devotion to the Italian tradition has brought him into closer relationship to the Neo-Romantic artists, particularly Bérard, Berman and Tchelitchew, whose own inspiration has so often derived from Italian sources. The signs of this kinship have, however, been long developing. To the post-abstract vocabulary of Parisian painting, both the Surrealists and the Neo-Romantics have from the beginning contributed, and from it both groups have drawn freely. The vocabulary's terminology is Romantic, although it has largely escaped the cumbrance of literary conceit which finally reduced the nineteenth century Romantic tradition to pedantry. Through it have been re-stated, among other things, the imaginative elegance and fantasy upon which the Cubists had turned their backs, following the lead of Cézanne, whom Dali was characteristically to dismiss as a "platonic mason" (bibl. 36). And if Dali has given the new vocabulary much of its vigor and been accountable for its extravagance of phrase and use of *double entendre*, he has lately been impressed by the scholarly terms of the Neo-Romantics. In recent years he has deeply admired the works of Christian Bérard which, although few in number, have earned Bérard an enigmatic, central position in recent Parisian art, similar to that which Marcel Duchamp held earlier in the century. The head of the principal figure in Dali's *The triumph of Nautilus* (page 75) seems specifically based upon the heads in Bérard's wash drawings. The elegiac grace of the figures and the inclusion of architectural fragments in *Old age, adolescence, infancy* may be ascribed partially to the influence of Bérard and Berman. Yet it must immediately be said that Dali's impact upon the Neo-Romantics may be just as precisely measured. The truth of the matter is that in contributing mutually to the post-abstract vocabulary, Dali and the Neo-Romantics have tended to lessen the contradiction in their respective means of expression.

27

Whereas Dali was once partially somnambulist in inspiration and the Neo-Romantics were by comparison naturalist, now all have progressed to a ground which becomes increasingly common to all. The difference between *Accommodations of desire* (page 35) and a typical Neo-Romantic painting of 1929 was almost irreconcilable. Between *Old age, adolescence, infancy* and certain Neo-Romantic works of today it is a difference of vision and temperament rather than a basic difference of kind.

With the *Family of marsupial centaurs* (page 76) the evolution of Dali's ideology appears to have come full circle. For the painting summarizes in extreme degree the artist's decision TO BECOME CLASSIC, as the foreword to his recent exhibition proclaimed in bold type, to paint pictures "uniquely consecrated to the architecture of the Renaissance and to the Special Sciences" (bibl. 62). As even the most casual observer will note, the painting's composition is rigidly based on intersecting diagonals which divide the picture space into four equilateral triangles. The disposition of forms is regulated with forethought and certainty, and not a single gesture or wayward line is allowed to break the pattern of triangles and parallels. Whereas a few years previously Dali had shown his contempt for the classic formulas of composition by balancing the heavy left section of *Inventions of the monsters* with an almost invisible blue dog in the right foreground, he now reverted to the most sacrosanct rules of symmetry. *Family of marsupial centaurs* is plainly in full reaction against his earlier works wherein composition was avowedly determined by subconscious inspiration and based on the asymmetric laws of accident.

If the tendency exhibited in *Family of marsupial centaurs* is to be continued—and there is as yet no evidence one way or the other—then Dali's whole program is in need of drastic revision. The change in direction, if it proves permanent, will not have come without warning. To anyone at all familiar with Surrealist activity over the past five years, it has been clear that the bonds between Dali and the Surrealist movement have been wearing thin. For while the Surrealists have continued to concern themselves with revelations of subconscious thought and have reposed their hopes on group effort, Dali has year by year moved nearer a conscious objectivity, the focal point of which has been, perhaps inevitably, himself. The Surrealists have consequently rejected as impure and egocentric the obsessions which Dali has recorded primarily because they proceed from an intensely private megalomania in which he has great faith. It was Dali the solitary "madman" rather than Dali the Surrealist who recently wrote: "The two luckiest things that can happen to a contemporary painter are: first to be Spanish, and second to be named Dali. Both have happened to me" (bibl. 62). Now that war has disrupted Surrealism as a formal movement, Dali may perhaps allow his inspiration to rise nearer and nearer the surface of his mind, where dwells reason, the mortal enemy of the subconscious.

Whether he would be apt to let this happen without having had the blessing of Surrealism's greatest hero, Sigmund Freud, is an intricate problem. But shortly before Freud's death Dali met him in London and heard him say: "What interests me in your art is not the unconscious but the conscious." Although this had been more and more what interested Dali himself, he may understandably have taken final courage from Freud's pronouncement. He may then and there have determined to paint a picture such as *Family of marsupial centaurs*. When he did so, for whatever

28

reason, he inevitably reversed the whole Surrealist tendency and brought it back near its starting point. For whereas the Surrealists had eagerly brushed aside conscious thought in order to peer into the dark wells of the subconscious, Dali was now ready to scrutinize his subconscious for signs it might contain of conscious reason. When these signs appeared, as they so plainly did in *Family of marsupial centaurs*, he hailed them with much the same enthusiasm the Surrealists had shown when they had first plumbed the subconscious and found images of astonishing beauty. *Family of marsupial centaurs*, then, may be taken as the first concrete step in a new direction. Whether the direction will, if continued, prove fruitful or disastrous cannot fairly be judged from this one painting. We must wait and see, remembering that among artists, integrity of hand is frequently more important than constancy of heart, as perhaps Dali intended to point out when he recently quoted Ingres' dictum, "Drawing is the integrity of art" (bibl. 62).

Whatever the future's judgment of Dali may be, it cannot be based solely on his accomplishments as a painter. From the very beginning of his career, he has striven to revive the Renaissance ideal of the artist as a man whose talents are applicable to the whole problem of esthetics. He has, for instance, worked seriously and steadily as a writer. In doing so he has furnished one more indication of his reaction against the beliefs of the older modern artists. Among leaders of the first School of Paris generation, only Rouault and de Chirico have consistently practiced literature, while Matisse, Braque and, until recently, Picasso have strictly and purposefully confined their expression to the plastic arts. Dali, on the other hand, has already completed an impressive list of poems, prose pieces and articles (see bibl.). In contrast to his elders, who have done their best to isolate their art from literary influences, he has gone so far as to write a poem (bibl. 22) to be played on a phonograph as the observer looks at his painting, *Narcissus*. There is additional proof of his desire to explore fields which the older Parisian painters have considered alien to their profession. While Matisse constantly attends the moving pictures in order to forget completely his labors as an artist, Dali regards the cinema as a medium for which he, as a painter, is ideally suited. He has collaborated with Luis Bunuel on the scenarios and direction of two films, *Un Chien Andalou* (1929) and *L'Âge d'Or* (1931).

Within the realm of the visual arts alone, Dali has ranged wider than members of the Picasso generation. He has designed furniture and jewelry and collaborated with Schiaparelli and Chanel in creating fashions, all in addition to the tasks of mural decoration and theater design in which his elders have also at various times been absorbed. His widespread activity may be ascribed partially to his connection with Surrealism, since that movement has discouraged the close devotion to métier in which Derain, for instance, has believed no less passionately than did Renoir. Following the lead of Marcel Duchamp, and to a lesser degree of Picasso, the Surrealists have attempted to show that art objects or anti-art objects may rival easel paintings in emotional force and validity, and Dali has consequently created innumerable articles from all manner of material, most of them reconstructions of dream imagery. They vary widely in size and intent, from an aphrodisiac smoking jacket to the famous raining taxi in which sat Columbus, whom Dali believes to have been a paranoiac, because in insisting that the world was round and hence endless, he betrayed a fear that he might be cornered by imaginary pursuers.

29

Since 1936 Dali's interest in the minor arts may have been further stimulated by his respect for the accomplishments of the Pre-Raphaelites. This interest has, of course, been shared by a few younger Surrealists and by the Neo-Romantics, among artists primarily associated with art activity centered in Paris. But only Dali has been willing to claim for his work in minor media an importance equal to that of his painting. While the others have quite understandably wished to be judged first of all as painters and sculptors, Dali has at times defended his art objects as against his own canvases. Surely he alone could say in all seriousness, as he recently did, "Cellini was a much greater artist than Michelangelo."

This review of Dali's career to date has purposefully been restricted to a discussion of the painter's technical and ideological development. The question of his position in contemporary art is at least partially answered by the indubitable fact that he is the most famous of the younger artists and that his influence, whether negatively or positively, has been widely felt. Perhaps this question may not now be answered more exactly. Even now, however, it seems clear that Dali has brought to a head the particular kind of anti-abstract revolt which had begun five years before his arrival in Paris among younger Parisian artists taking their direction from the early period of Giorgio de Chirico. If only because he is the *dernier cri*, Dali has to a certain extent replaced Picasso as a force to be accepted or dismissed in Parisian art. In England and America as well he has helped restore representational painting in general, and objective exactitude of technique in particular, to a favor which they might have rewon more slowly without him. The success of the reaction against abstract art for which he stands has not been complete in that the abstract movement continues to thrive, nourished on Picasso's boundless energy, Mondrian's dogma and Miro's inventiveness. But the reaction has at least succeeded in establishing itself on a basis of equal importance in contemporary esthetics.

There is a problem related solely to Dali's emergence as a public figure which deserves some comment. Is he an isolated phenomenon projected into fame by an unusual technique, a weird imagination and a flair for publicity? Or does he reflect, in exaggerated form, the psychology of his epoch? Is he pure eccentric or part prophet? Although parallels between an artist and his time are frequently of dubious validity when drawn by a contemporary, there are a few in Dali's case which at least carry the weight of plausible conjecture.

To begin with, even the most determined Narcissus cannot isolate his own image, and the pool into which Dali has stared so fixedly carries reflections of his surroundings that no flurry of pebbles can dispel. His identification with Surrealism, which to many once signified a childish retreat from reality, may now conceivably be re-read as a passionate espousal of a counter-reality to which all France, all civilized Europe, had been clinging for assurance. The double image no longer appears so personal a device in a world where statesmen as well as painters portray objectives with such cunning that they become "without the slightest physical or anatomical change, the representation of another entirely different object, the second representation being equally devoid of any deformation or abnormality betraying arrangement." In view of the frightful havoc which machines have lately wrought on earth, one may properly inquire whether

30

Dali's loathing of them has been merely egocentric and exhibitionistic. To narrow the question, one may ask which type of architecture more accurately diagnosed the hidden psychosis of the years just before the present war: *machines à habiter*, with their flat white roofing and broad areas of glass; or the small, dark, womblike houses which Dali proposed to build as retreats from a mechanical civilization and which now, as portable air raid shelters, cover the landscape of England.

That the era in which Dali has come to fame has been one of immense neuroticism, few will any longer deny. It has been an era of stepped-up emotion, of restlessness and phobias to which artists, having figuratively one less layer of skin than laymen, have naturally been sensitive. The anatomy of the era has been an anatomy of nerves, its spiritual regeneration reduced to therapeutic measures. In America, where Dali's fame has been the greatest, large sections of the public have acquired a taste for vicariously experiencing all manner of violent sensations. The tabloids, radio and moving pictures have fed the taste with a cunning hand, and in vast numbers of people a ferocious appetite for the morbid has been induced which only the horror of war seems likely to bring to prime satiety. The question inevitably arises: in paying heed to Dali, has the epoch been paying heed to itself?

To suggest the maximum significance of Dali's hold on popular consciousness is not to preclude the chance that this significance may be less deeply rooted than certain parallels indicate. The matter of intrinsic worth aside, fame has often come to artists for reasons which history has gone halt pursuing. It may be that Dali is an isolated phenomenon, for whom Freud's epithet, "What a fanatic!" is apt and final, as Dali has proudly proclaimed it. If this be true, then to Dali must be said what Victor Hugo respectfully wrote to no less a poet than Charles Baudelaire: "You create a new shudder."

JAMES THRALL SOBY

BRIEF CHRONOLOGY

1904   Salvador Dali born in Figueras, Spain.

Early   Admired 17th-century Dutch still-life
youth   painters, 19th-century Spanish painters
of genre scenes and the French Impres-
sionists.
Studied intermittently at the Madrid
School of Fine Arts (c. 1921–1926).

c. 1921   Influenced by Italian Futurism.

1923–1925   Painted under influence of "Metaphysical
School" of Italian artists (1915–1920),
among them Giorgio de Chirico and Carlo
Carrà.

1925–1928   Abstract period. Influenced in turn by
Cézanne, Picasso, Miro. Executed Cubist
works.

1929   Began painting literal transcriptions of his
dreams (summer).
Moved to Paris and became an official
Surrealist (fall).
First Paris exhibition, Galerie Goemans.
Made film, *Un Chien Andalou*, with Bunuel.

1929–1931   Influenced by early period of Giorgio de
Chirico, by Max Ernst, Yves Tanguy and
art nouveau decoration and furniture.

1929–1933   Inspired by Arcimboldo and Bracelli, began painting double images in *The invisible man*.

1930   Published *La femme visible*, giving his
theories of "paranoiac" inspiration.
Called his technique "handmade photography," related it to that of Meissonier.

1930–1934   Paintings reflected his obsession with a
Freudian conception of the legend of
William Tell and, slightly later, of *The
Angelus* of Millet.

1931   Made film, *L' Âge d'Or*, with Bunuel.

1933   First New York one-man show, Julien
Levy Gallery.

1933–1934   "Bone" series; figures with cephalic deformations.

1934   First visit to the United States; arrived
November 14.

1934–1936   Beach scenes at Rosas (Spain), with "instantaneous" figures.

1936   Decorations for the residence of Edward
James, London.

1937–1939   Increasingly admired Vermeer and Velasquez.
Three extended visits to Italy brought
him new appreciation of Italian Baroque
painting: Caravaggio, the *tenebrosi*, Magnasco.

1939   Designed and supervised construction of
Dali's Dream House, erected in amuse-
ment area of the World's Fair, New York.
Wrote book, designed costumes and décor
for the ballet *Bacchanale*.

1940   Arrived in the United States August 16.

1941   Wrote book, designed costumes and décor
for the ballet *Labyrinth*.

PLATES

1. Still Life. 1924. Oil on canvas. Private collection. *Not included in exhibition.*

2. Harlequin. Ca. 1925. Oil on canvas, ca. 8 x 6 feet. Collection of the artist. *Not included in exhibition.*

3. The basket of bread. 1926. Oil on panel, 14 x 13¾ inches. Private Collection.

4. Illumined pleasures. 1929. Oil on panel, 9⅜ x 13⅝ inches. Collection Sidney Janis.

5. Accommodations of desire. 1929. Oil on panel, 8⅝ x 13¾ inches. Collection Julien Levy.

6. The invisible man. 1929–33 (incomplete state). Oil on canvas. Collection Vicomte Charles de Noailles. *Not included in exhibition.*

36

7. The font. 1930. Oil on composition board, 26 x 16¼ inches.
Collection Edward Wassermann.

8. The feeling of becoming. 1930. Oil on canvas, 13¾ x 10⅝ inches. Collection Mrs. W. Murray Crane.

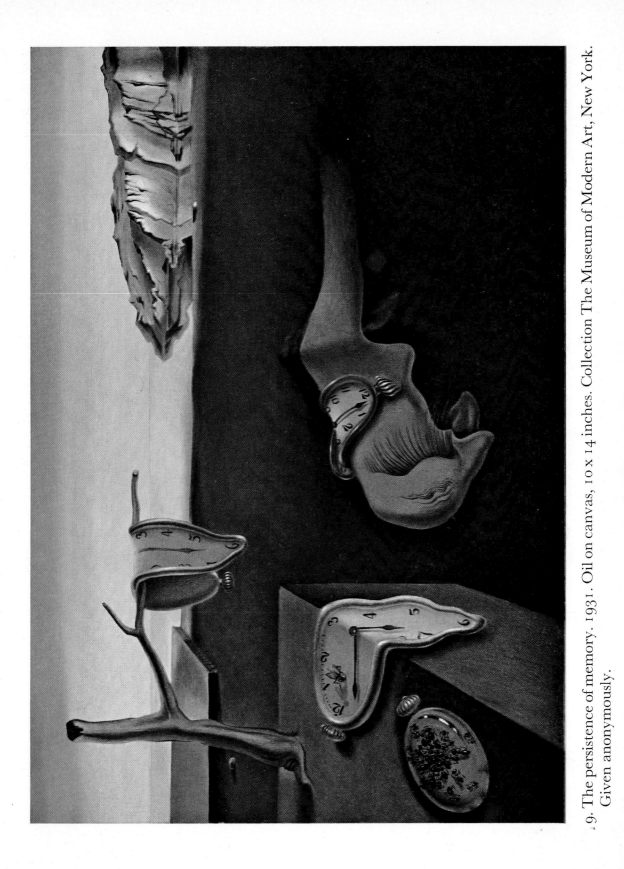

19. The persistence of memory. 1931. Oil on canvas, 10 x 14 inches. Collection The Museum of Modern Art, New York. Given anonymously.

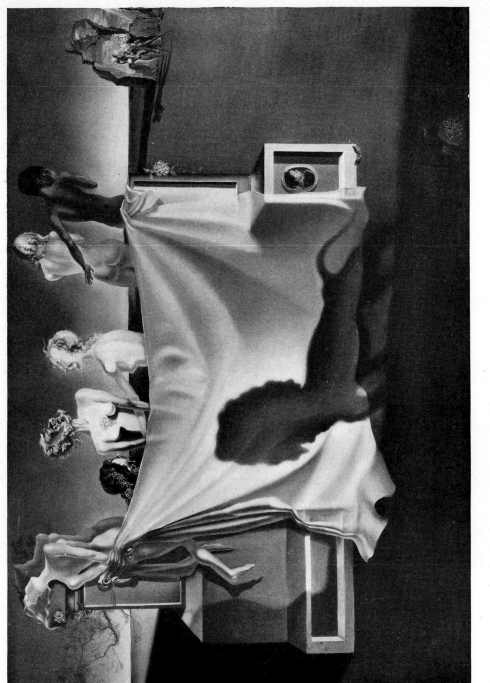

10. The old age of William Tell. 1931. Oil on canvas. Collection Vicomte Charles de Noailles. *Not included in exhibition.*

11. Shades of night descending. 1931. Oil on canvas, 24 x 19¾ inches. Collection
The Art Institute of Chicago.

12. Agnostic symbol. 1932. Oil on
canvas, 26¾ x 25¼ inches.
Collection Mr. and Mrs. Walter C. Arensberg.

13. Myself at the age of ten when
I was the grasshopper child.
1933. Oil on panel, 8⅞ x 6¾
inches. Collection Joseph Cornell.

14. The phantom cart. 1933. Oil on panel, 6 x 8½ inches. Collection Thomas Fine Howard.

44

15. Gala and the Angelus of Millet immediately preceding the arrival of the conic anamorphoses. 1933. Oil on panel, 9⅜ x 7⅜ inches.
Collection Henry P. McIlhenny.

16. Javanese mannequin. 1933–34. Oil on canvas, 25 x 21 inches. Collection Julien Levy.

17. The spectre of sex appeal. 1934. Oil on panel, 7 x 5½ inches. Collection of the artist.

48

18. Average atmospherocephalic bureaucrat in the act of milking a cranial harp. 1934. Oil on canvas, 8¾ x 6½ inches. Collection of the artist.

19. Aerodynamic chair. 1934. Oil on panel, 8⅝ x 6¼ inches. Collection
De Beers Consolidated Mines, Ltd.

20. Symbol of anguish. 1934. Oil on panel, 8¾ x 6⅜ inches. Collection
Mrs. Irving T. Snyder.

21. Enigmatic elements in a landscape. 1934. Oil on panel, $28\frac{5}{8}$ x $23\frac{1}{2}$ inches. Collection The International Business Machines Corp.

52

22. The ghost of Vermeer of Delft, which can be used as a table. 1934. Oil on panel, 7⅛ x 5½ inches. Private collection.

23. Cardinal, cardinal! 1934. Oil on panel, 6⅜ x 8⅝ inches.
Collection Julien Levy.

24. The weaning of furniture-nutrition. 1934. Oil on canvas.
Collection Jocelyn Walker. *Not included in the exhibition.*

25. Paranoiac-astral image. 1934. Oil on panel, 6¼ x 8⅝ inches. Collection The Wadsworth Atheneum, Hartford.

26. Portrait of Gala. 1935. Oil on panel, 12¾ x 10½ inches. Collection The
Museum of Modern Art, New York. Given anonymously.

27. Nostalgic echo. 1935. Oil on canvas, 38¼ x 38¼ inches. Collection Dr. and Mrs. Leslie M. Maitland.

28. Noon. 1936. Oil on canvas, $35\frac{3}{8}$ x $45\frac{1}{2}$ inches. Collection Mrs. John Pitney.

29. A chemist lifting with extreme precaution the cuticle of a grand piano. 1936.
Oil on canvas, 19¾ x 25½ inches. Collection Miss Ruth Page.

30. The man with the head of blue hortensias. 1936. Oil on canvas,
6⅜ x 8⅝ inches. Private collection.

31. Three young surrealist women holding in their arms the
skins of an orchestra. 1936. Oil on canvas, 21¼ x 25⅝
inches. Collection Thomas A. Fransioli, Jr.

60

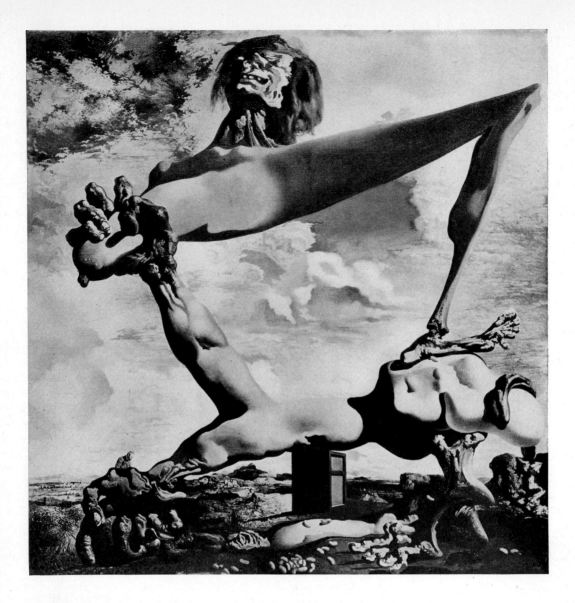

32. Soft construction with boiled beans; premonition of civil war. 1936. Oil on canvas, 39½ x 39½ inches. Collection Mr. and Mrs. Walter C. Arensberg.

33. Inventions of the monsters. 1937. Oil on canvas, 20⅛ x 30⅞ inches. Private collection.

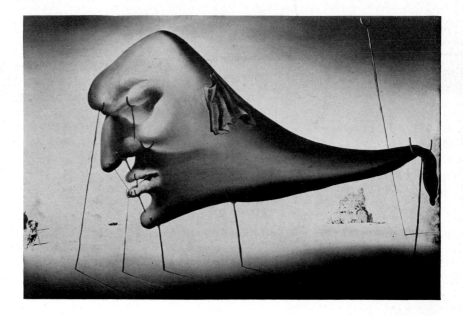

34. Sleep. 1937. Oil on canvas, 20 x 30¾ inches. Collection Edward James.

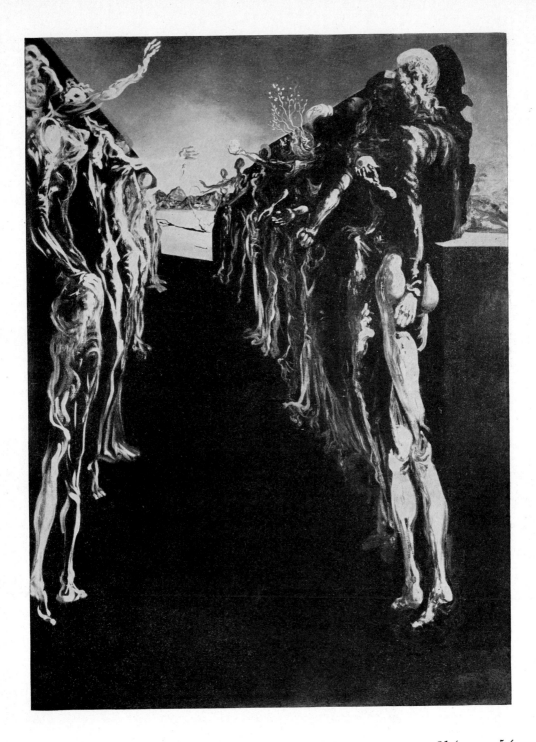

35. Palladio's corridor of Thalia. 1937. Oil on canvas, 46¼ x 35⅝ inches. Collection Edward James.

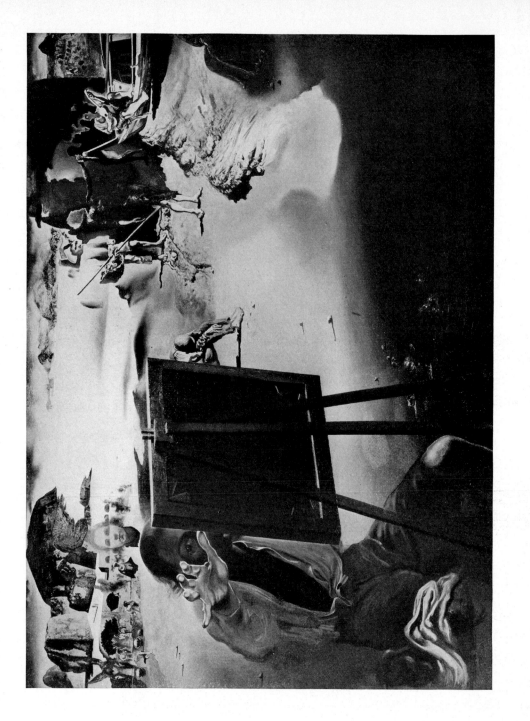

36. Impression of Africa. 1938. Oil on canvas, 36 x 46¼ inches. Collection Edward James.

37. The sublime moment. 1938. Oil on canvas, 15½ x 18½ inches. Collection of the artist.

38. Imperial violets. 1938. Oil on canvas, 39¼ x 56⅛ inches. Collection The Museum of Modern Art, New York. Gift of Edward James.

39. Debris of an automobile giving birth to a blind horse biting a telephone.
1938. Oil on canvas, 21¼ x 25½ inches. Private collection.

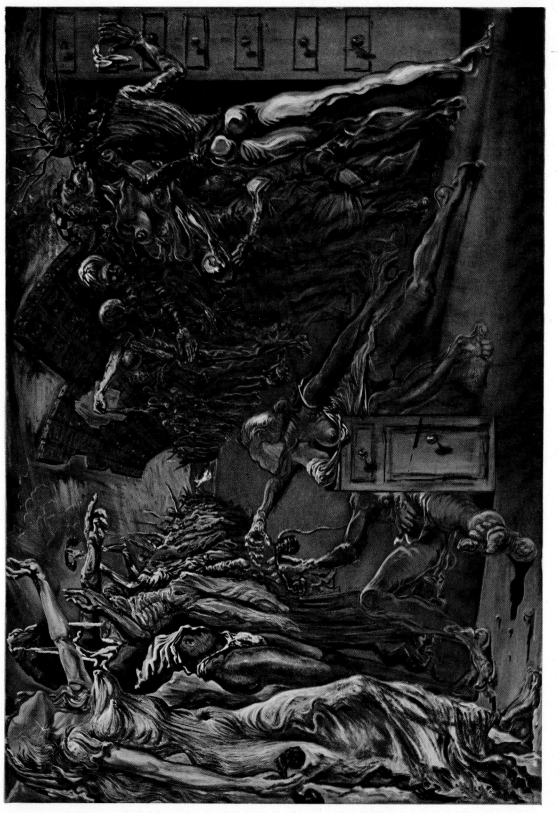

40. Palladio's corridor of dramatic surprise. 1938. Oil on canvas, 28¾ x 41 inches. Collection Mr. and Mrs. R. Kirk Askew, Jr.

41. Apparition of face and fruit-dish on a beach. 1938. Oil on canvas, 45 x 57½ inches. Collection The Wadsworth Atheneum, Hartford.

42. Psychoanalysis and morphology meet. 1939. Oil on canvas, 10 x 18⅜ inches. Collection Mrs. Gerard B. Lambert.

43. Enchanted beach with three fluid graces. 1938-39. Oil on canvas, 25½ x 31½ inches. Collection of the artist.

41. Philosophy illuminated by the light of the moon and the setting sun. 1939. Oil on canvas, 51 x 64 inches. Collection of the artist.

45. Group of women imitating the gestures of a schooner. 1940. Oil on canvas,
21½ x 25¾ inches. Collection Mrs. Harold McCormick.

46. Two pieces of bread expressing the sentiment of love. 1940. Oil on canvas, 32¼ x 39½ inches. Collection of the artist.

47. Two pieces of bread expressing the sentiment of love. (*detail.*)

48. Old age, adolescence, infancy. 1940. Oil on canvas, $19\frac{5}{8}$ x $25\frac{5}{8}$ inches. Collection of the artist.

49. The triumph of Nautilus. 1941. Oil on canvas, 11⅛ x 13⅞ inches. Collection
Miss Vera Zorina.

50. Family of marsupial centaurs. 1941. Oil on canvas. Collection of the artist.
Not included in exhibition.

76

51. Second surrealist manifesto. 1930. Ink and water color, 12 x 10¾ inches. Collection Sidney Janis.

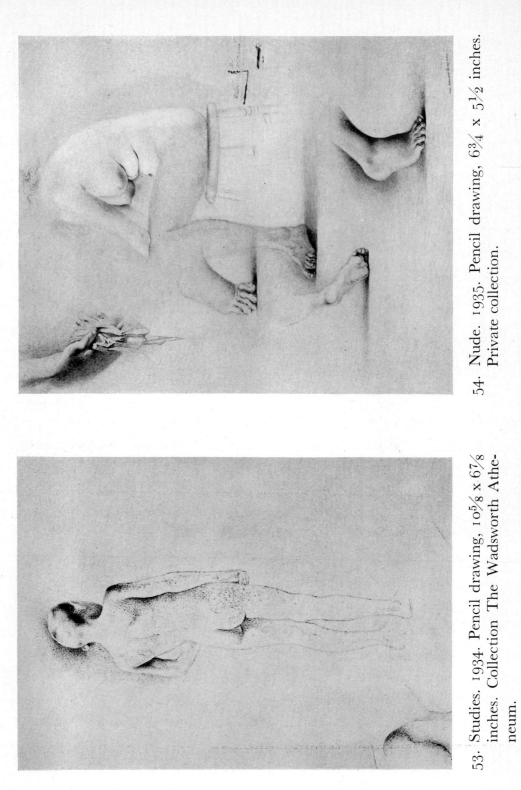

54. Nude. 1935. Pencil drawing, 6¾ x 5½ inches. Private collection.

53. Studies. 1934. Pencil drawing, 10⅝ x 6⅞ inches. Collection The Wadsworth Atheneum.

78

54. Anthropomorphic echo. 1936. Ink and pencil, 20½ x 17 inches. Collection Mrs. G. Reginald Monkhouse.

55. Study of horsemen. 1936. Ink drawing, 17 x 21 inches. Collection The Museum of Modern Art, New York. Gift of Sam A. Lewisohn.

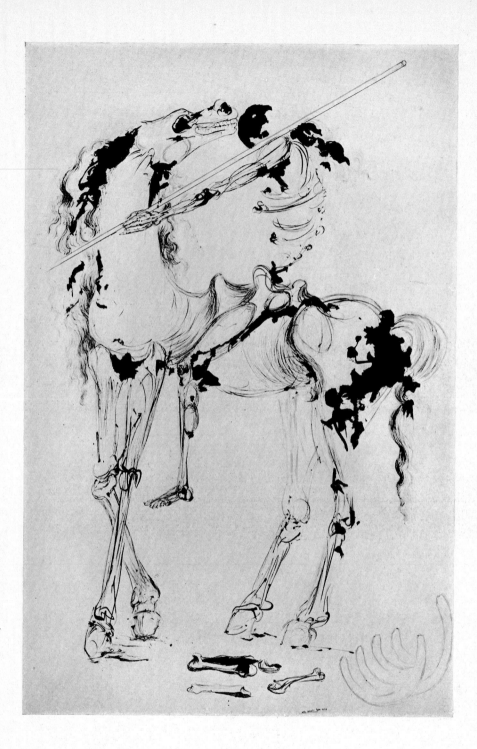

56. Cavalier of death. 1936. Ink drawing, 33½ x 22⅜ inches.
Collection Mrs. Stanley Resor.

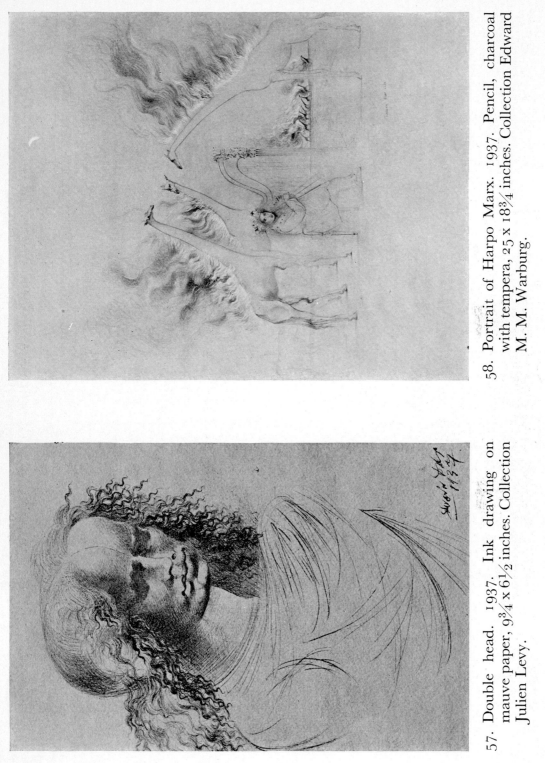

58. Portrait of Harpo Marx. 1937. Pencil, charcoal with tempera, 25 x 18¾ inches. Collection Edward M. M. Warburg.

57. Double head. 1937. Ink drawing on mauve paper, 9¾ x 6½ inches. Collection Julien Levy.

81

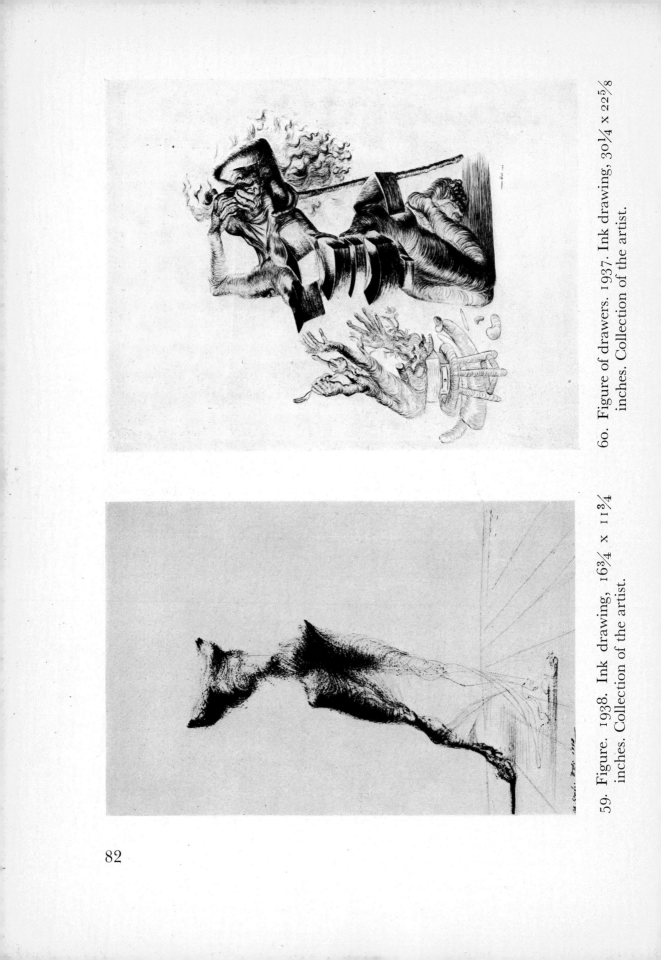

60. Figure of drawers. 1937. Ink drawing, 30¼ x 22⅝ inches. Collection of the artist.

59. Figure. 1938. Ink drawing, 16¾ x 11¾ inches. Collection of the artist.

82

61. Marsupial figure. 1940. Ink drawing,
27¼ x 21¾ inches. Collection of the artist.

62. Hysterical arch. 1937. Ink drawing, 22 x 30⅛ inches. Collection of the artist.

DRAWINGS BY DALI

Included in the exhibition but not illustrated in the catalog.

Andromeda. 1931. Pencil drawing, 28 x 21 inches. Collection A. Conger Goodyear.

The convalescence of a kleptomaniac. 1933. Pencil and ink, 19¾ x 14 inches. Collection Mrs. W. Murray Crane.

The inaccessible hour. 1936. Ink drawing, 21¼ x 17¼ inches. Collection Mrs. George Waller Blow.

Harpo Marx. 1937. Pencil drawing, 16¼ x 12¾ inches. Collection Henry P. McIlhenny.

Nude. 1939. Ink drawing on mauve paper, 16¾ x 23 inches. Collection Allen Porter.

JEWELRY BY DALI

Designed in collaboration with the Duke di Verdura.

Cigarette box. 1941. Pale gold with jewelled beetle and painting on ivory. Lent by Mrs. David M. Levy.

Apollo and Daphne. 1941. Brooch, oil on gold, pink tourmaline; frame: gold, rubies, turquoises, 3 inches high. Lent by Verdura, Inc.

Head of Medusa. 1941. Brooch, oil on gold, Morganite, gold, rubies, 2½ inches wide. Lent by Verdura, Inc.

St. Sebastian. 1941. Object, oil on gold, petrified wood, agate, rubies, 5½ inches high. Lent by Verdura, Inc.

Angel. 1941. Box, tourmaline, oil on ivory, gold, 2⅛ x 1⅝ inches. Lent by Verdura, Inc.

Shell brooch with gold and diamonds. 1941. 3½ inches wide. Lent by Verdura, Inc.

BALLETS IN WHICH DALI HAS COLLABORATED

Bacchanale

Ballet in one act. Book: Salvador Dali. Music: Richard Wagner (the Venusberg from *Tannhäuser*). Choreography: Léonide Massine. Scenery and costumes: Salvador Dali. First produced: Metropolitan Opera House, New York, November 9, 1939.

Labyrinth

Ballet in one act. Book: Salvador Dali. Music: Franz Schubert (Seventh Symphony in C Major). Choreography: Léonide Massine. Scenery and costumes: Salvador Dali. First produced: Metropolitan Opera House, New York, October 8, 1941.

FILMS BY DALI AND BUNUEL

Un chien andalou. Scenario by Salvador Dali and Luis Bunuel; produced and directed by Luis Bunuel. Paris 1929.

L'Âge d'Or. Scenario by Salvador Dali and Luis Bunuel; produced and directed by Luis Bunuel. Paris 1931.

ONE-MAN EXHIBITIONS OF DALI'S WORK

1929 PARIS, Galerie Goemans—Nov. 20–Dec. 5

1930 PARIS, Galerie Pierre Colle

1931 PARIS, Galerie Pierre Colle—June 3–15

1932 PARIS, Galerie Pierre Colle—May 26–June 17

1933 NEW YORK, Julien Levy Gallery—Nov. 21–Dec. 12

1934 NEW YORK, Julien Levy Gallery—Apr. 3—(drawings and etchings to illustrate *Les chants de Maldoror*)

1934 PARIS, Galerie Jacques Bonjean—June 20–July 14

1934 LONDON, Zwemmer Gallery

1934 BARCELONA, Galeries d'art Catalonia—Oct. 2–4

1934 NEW YORK, Julien Levy Gallery—Nov. 21–Dec. 10

1936 LONDON, Alex. Reid and Lefevre, Ltd.—June–July

1937 NEW YORK, Julien Levy Gallery—Dec. 15, 1936–Jan. 15

1939 PARIS, An exhibition in the artist's apartment—February

1939 NEW YORK, Julien Levy Gallery—Mar. 21–Apr. 18

1939 NEW YORK, World's Fair, The Dream of Venus—June–Oct.

1941 NEW YORK, Julien Levy Gallery—Apr. 22–May 31

1941 CHICAGO, The Arts Club of Chicago—May 23–June 14

1941 LOS ANGELES, Dalzell Hatfield Galleries—Sept. 10–Oct. 5

BIBLIOGRAPHY

This bibliography is divided into three parts: nos. 1–39, LITERATURE BY DALI; nos. 40–70, LITERATURE ON DALI; nos. 71–82, ILLUSTRATION BY DALI. The arrangement is alphabetical, under the author's name wherever possible. Catalogs of exhibitions in public museums are listed under the name of the city where the museum is located, while private exhibition galleries are listed under the name of the gallery. The bibliographical form is modelled upon that used by the Art Index.

ABBREVIATIONS. Ap *April*, Ag *August*, D *December*, ed *editor*, –ion, F *February*, Ja *January*, Je *June*, Jl *July*, Mr *March*, My *May*, N *November*, no *number*, O *October*, p *page(s)*, S *September*.

SAMPLE ENTRY for magazine article: The object as revealed in surrealist experiment. This Quarter 5no1:197–207 S 1932.

EXPLANATION. An article entitled "The Object as Revealed in Surrealist Experiment," will be found in This Quarter, volume 5, number 1, pages 197 to 207 inclusive, the September, 1932 issue.

LITERATURE BY DALI

1. L'amour et la mémoire. Paris, Éd. Surréalistes, 1931.
   Translated on p145–6 of item 54, below; also on p158–9 of item 61.
2. L'âne pourri. Le Surréalisme au Service de la Révolution no1:9–12 1930.
   Translated in 35.
3. The Angelus of Millet. The New Hope 2no4:10,21,24 Ag 1934.
   Translated by Samuel Putnam.
4. Apparitions aérodynamiques des "Êtres-objets." Minotaure no6:33–4 1935.
5. Babaouo; scenario inédit. Précédé d'un abrégé d'une histoire critique du cinéma, et suivi de Guillaume Tell, ballet portugais. Paris, Éd. des Cahiers Libres, 1932.
6. Binding cradles—cradle bound [poem]. In: J. Levy, Surrealism. p157. New York, Black Sun Press, 1936.

7. Communication: Visage paranoïaque. Le Surréalisme au Service de la Révolution no3:[40] 1931.
8. Conquest of the irrational. New York, J. Levy, 1935.
9. Dali, Dali! In: catalog of Dali exhibition, Julien Levy Gallery, New York, 1939.
10. De la beauté terrifiante et comestible de l'architecture modern' style. Minotaure no3–4:69–76 1933.
11. Declaration of the independence of the imagination and the rights of man to his own madness. 4p [New York, privately published, 1939].
    Partially reprinted in Art Digest 13:9 Ag 1939.
12. Derniers modes d'excitation intellectuelle pour l'été 1934. Documents 34 new series no1:33–35 Je 1934.
13. Dictionnaire abrégé du surréalisme. Paris, Galerie Beaux-Arts, 1938.
    With numerous definitions by Dali.
14. [Discussion of his own art.] In: E. Tériade, Emancipation de la peinture. Minotaure no3–4:18,20 1933.
15. Du temps que les surréalistes avaient raison. Paris, Éd. Surréalistes, 1935.
    Articles signed by Dali, Breton, Eluard, Ernst, and others.
16. Les eaux où nous nageons. Cahiers d'Art 10 no5–6:122–4 1935.
    Translated in 8 p7–11.
17. La femme visible. Paris, Éd. Surréalistes, 1930.
18. Geological foundations of Venusberg, 1939. In: Program of the Metropolitan Opera House, New York, April 6, 1940.
19. Honneur à l'objet! Cahiers d'Art 11no 1–2:53–6 1936.
20. Les idées lumineuses. Cahiers d'Art 15 no1–2:24–5 1940.
21. Interprétation paranoïaque—critique de l'image obsédante "L'Angelus" de Millet. Minotaure no1:65–7 1933.
22. La métamorphose de Narcisse; poème paranoïaque. Paris, Éd. Surréalistes, 1936.
    English translation by Francis Scarpe, New York, J. Levy, 1937.

23. Notes—communications. Le Surréalisme au Service de la Révolution no6:40–41 1933.

24. Notes pour l'interprétation du tableau "La persistence de la mémoire." Manuscript: photostat in Library of the Museum of Modern Art.

25. Les nouvelles couleurs du sex appeal spectral. Minotaure no5:20–2 1934.

26. The object as revealed in surrealist experiment. This Quarter 5no1:197–207 S 1932.

27. Objets psycho-atmosphériques anamorphiques. Le Surréalisme au Service de la Révolution no5:45–8 1933.

28. Objets surréalistes. Le Surréalisme au Service de la Révolution no3:16–17 1931.

29. Les pantoufles de Picasso. Cahiers d'Art 10 no7–10:208–12 1935.

30. Le phénomène de l'extase. Minotaure no3–4:76–7 1933.

31. Première loi morphologique sur les poils dans les structures molles. Minotaure no9:60–1 1936.

32. Psychologie non-euclidienne d'une photographie. Minotaure no7:56–7 1935.

33. Rêverie. Le Surréalisme au Service de la Révolution no4:31–6 1931.

34. The secret life of Salvador Dali. Town & Country 96:54–7,94,96–8 My 1941.
    Excerpts from the forthcoming autobiography.

35. The stinking ass. This Quarter 5no1:49–54 S 1932.

36. Le surréalisme spectral de l'éternel féminin préraphaélite. Minotaure no8:46–9 1936.

WITH LUIS BUNUEL

37. Un chien andalou. La Révolution Surréaliste no12:34–7 D 15 1929.
    Scenario of a film. Translation: "The Andalusian Dog," in This Quarter, 5no1:149–57 S 1932.

38. L'âge d'or. Paris, Corti, 1931.
    Scenario of a film.

WITH RENÉ CREVEL

39. Per un tribunal terrorista de responsabili-

tats intelectuals. Barcelona, La Hora, 1931.

LITERATURE ON DALI

40. American cult for surrealism: Dali. Art News 35:17 Ja 2 1937.

41. ARAGON, LOUIS. La peinture au défi. p27–8. Paris, Corti, 1930.

42. BATAILLE, G. Le jeu lugubre. Documents no7:369–72 D 1929.

43. BOR, VANE. Correspondance à Salvador Dali. Le Surréalisme au Service de la Révolution no6:46–7 1933.

44. BOSWELL, PEYTON, JR. Is Dali crazy? Art Digest 15:3 My 1 1941.

45. BRETON, ANDRÉ. Introduction to catalog of Dali exhibition, Galerie Goemans, Paris, N 20–D 5 1929.
    Translated into English as "The first Dali exhibition," in A. Breton, What is Surrealism? p27–30 (No 46, below).

46. ———. What is surrealism? p27–30,82–4 London, Faber & Faber, 1936.

47. CALAS, NICOLAS. Anti-surrealist Dali: I say his flies are ersatz. View (New York) 1no6:1,3 Je 1941.

48. CASSOU, JEAN. La jeune peinture espagnol. Renaissance 16:162–3 Jl 1933.

49. CHERONNET, LOUIS. Salvador Dali. Art et Décoration 63:280 Jl 1934.

50. CREVEL, RENÉ. Dali; ou, L'anti-obscurantisme. Paris, Éd. Surréalistes, 1931.

51. CURRENT BIOGRAPHY 1:219–21 1940.
    Biographical sketch.

52. DOMINGUEZ, OSCAR. Carta de Paris; conversación con Salvador Dali. Gaceta de Arte (Tenerife, Canary Islands) 3no28:3 1934.

53. Frozen nightmares. Time 24no22:44–5 N 26 1934.

54. GASCOYNE, DAVID. A short survey of surrealism. London, Cobden-Sanderson, 1936.

55. GAUNT, W. Art's nightmare: the surrealist paintings of Salvador Dali. London Studio 18:108–13 S 1939.

56. GEORGE, WALDEMAR. Avant son départ pour New-York, Salvator [sic] Dali a presenté dans son atelier un choix de ses oeuvres. Beaux Arts p4 F 10 1939.

57. HARRIMAN, MARGARET CASE. Profiles: A dream walking. The New Yorker 15:22–7 Jl 1 1939.

58. HILAIRE, G. Chez les surréalistes: Salvador Dali. Beaux Arts p2 Je 30 1933.

59. HUYGHE, RENÉ, ed. Histoire de l'art contemporain: la peinture. Paris, Alcan, 1935.
   Biographical and bibliographical note, p343, reprinted from L'Amour de L'Art 15:343 Mr 1934.
   JACINTO, FELIPE. See 62.

60. LAPRADE, J. DE. Salvador Dali. Beaux Arts p1 Je 19 1934.

61. LEVY, JULIEN. Surrealism. New York, Black Sun Press, 1936.

62. LEVY, JULIEN, GALLERY. Salvador Dali. Ap 22–My 31 1941.
   Exhibition catalog, with text "The last scandal of Salvador Dali" by Felipe Jacinto. Reissued, in slightly different form by the Arts Club of Chicago, and by Dalzell Hatfield Galleries, Los Angeles, to accompany their respective showings of the exhibition in 1941.

63. LOPEZ TORRES, DOMINGO. Lo real y lo superreal en la pintura de Salvador Dali. Gaceta de Arte (Tenerife, Canary Islands) no28:1–2 Jl 1934.

64. NICHOLS, D. Reply [to Dali manifesto, see 11 above]. Art Digest 13:26 S 1939.

64a. NEW YORK. THE MUSEUM OF MODERN ART. Fantastic art, dada, surrealism. Edited by Alfred H. Barr, Jr., and Georges Hugnet. 2d ed. 1937.

65. READ, HERBERT, ed. Surrealism. London, Faber & Faber, 1936.

66. SETON, MARIE. S. Dali + 3 Marxes = Theatre Arts Monthly 23:734–40 O 1939.

67. SOBY, JAMES THRALL. After Picasso. New York, Dodd, Mead, 1935.

68. STEUBEN GLASS, INC., NEW YORK. Collection of designs in glass by twenty-seven contemporary artists. 1940.
   Catalog of an exhibition. Illustration of Dali's work and biographical note.

69. WATT, A. Dali à Londres. Beaux Arts p1 N 30 1934.

70. WOOLF, S. J. Dali's doodles come to town. New York Times Magazine p11,16 Mr 12 1939.

ILLUSTRATION BY DALI

71. Un album de 6 photographies des tableaux de Salvador Dali. Paris, Corti, 1932.

72. New York as seen by the super-realist artist, M. Dali. American Weekly p3 F 24 1935.
   ". . . the sketches on this page . . . were made for The American Weekly."

73. How super-realist Dali saw Broadway. American Weekly p5 Mr 17 1935.
   A page of drawings made for the American Weekly.

74. [Cover] Minotaure no8 1936.

75. Original sketch . . . the under water dream house [at New York World's Fair]. Town & Country 94:46–47 Je 1939.
   Republished Town & Country 96:54–7 My 1941.

76. BRETON, ANDRÉ. Le revolver à cheveux blancs. Paris, Éd. des Cahiers Libres, 1932.
   An etching by Dali in each of 10 copies printed on Japan paper.

77. ———and Eluard, Paul. L'immaculée conception. Paris, Corti, 1930.

78. CHAR, RENÉ. Artine. Paris, Éd. Surréalistes, 1930.
   Nos 1–30 of the edition of 185 include an engraving by Dali.

79. DUCASSE, ISADORE [Comte de Lautréamont]. Les chants de Maldoror. Paris, Skira, 1934.
   Original etchings by Dali.

80. ELUARD, PAUL. Nuits partagées. Avec deux dessins par Salvador Dali. Paris, Éd. G.L.M., 1935.

81. HUGNET, GEORGES. Onan. Paris, Éd. Surréalistes, 1934.
   Original etching in nos 1–50 of 250 copies.

82. JAMES, EDWARD. Trois sécheresses. Minotaure no8:53–6 1936.
   4 illustrations by Dali.
   LAUTRÉAMONT, COMTE DE. See 79.

TEN THOUSAND COPIES OF THIS BOOK HAVE BEEN PRINTED IN NOVEMBER, 1941, FOR THE TRUSTEES OF THE MUSEUM OF MODERN ART BY THE PLANTIN PRESS, NEW YORK